No Alternative? Unemployment in Britain

Sean Glynn is Senior Lecturer in Economic and Social History at the University of Kent at Canterbury. He has published seven books and numerous articles, many of which deal with questions of unemployment and policy. His other books include *The Road to Full Employment*, *Interwar Britain*, *The State and Primary Production* and *Urbanisation in Australian History*.

NO ALTERNATIVE?
UNEMPLOYMENT IN BRITAIN

Sean Glynn

faber and faber
LONDON · BOSTON

First published in 1991
by Faber and Faber Limited
3 Queen Square London WCIN 3AU

Photoset by Wilmaset Birkenhead Wirral
Printed in England by
Clays Ltd, St Ives plc

© Sean Glynn, 1991

Sean Glynn is hereby identified as the author
of this work in accordance with Section 77 of the
Copyright, Design and Patents Act 1988.

A CIP record for this book
is available from the British Library

ISBN 0–571–14210–9

'O brave new world', said Robyn, 'where only the managing directors have jobs.'

This time Wilcox did not miss her irony.

'I don't like making men redundant,' he said, 'but we're caught in a double bind. If we don't modernise we lose competitive edge and have to make men redundant, and if we do modernise we have to make men redundant because we don't need 'em any more.'

'What we should be doing is spending more money preparing people for creative leisure,' said Robyn.

David Lodge, Nice Work (1988)

HISTORICAL HANDBOOKS

Series Editors:
Avner Offer – University of York
F. M. L. Thompson – Institute of Historical Research,
University of London

It is widely recognized that many of the problems of present-day society are deeply rooted in the past, but the actual lines of historical development are often known only to a few specialists, while the policy-makers and analysts themselves frequently rely on a simplified, dramatized, and misleading version of history. Just as the urban landscape of today was largely built in a world that is no longer familiar, so the policy landscape is shaped by attitudes and institutions formed under very different conditions in the past. This series of specially commissioned handbooks aims to provide short, up-to-date studies in the evolution of current problems, not in the form of narratives but as critical accounts of the ways in which the present is formed by the past, and of the roots of present discontents. Designed for those with little time for extensive reading in the specialized literature, the books contain bibliographies for further study. The authors aim to be as accurate and comprehensive as possible, but not anodyne; their arguments, forcefully expressed, make the historical experience available in challenging form, but do not presume to offer ready-made solutions.

Contents

Preface

This book is aimed at the general reader and the student rather than the specialist and it is designed to open up what has become a major subject in modern history and contemporary debate, as well as a basic issue in economics and other social sciences. Unemployment is a large and complex phenomenon which has generated a voluminous and rapidly growing literature. In dealing with unemployment one is inevitably concerned with a wide range of other important issues including economic and social policy, social security and political development, to mention only three. A short handbook such as this can aim to do no more than scratch the surface in what must, quite inevitably, be an inadequate effort. However, many of the omissions and deficiencies in what follows will be dealt with in a companion volume by Noel Whiteside which deals with the social aspects of unemployment. Also, the select bibliography will direct the reader to other general and also some specialist works.

In dealing historically with this important and highly controversial subject one becomes ever more aware of political falsehoods and hypocrisy over the decades alongside the amazing range of expert opinion which covers a very wide range of possibility. I hope that a sense of irony and moral outrage has been conveyed in the context of a genuine attempt to reflect, fairly and as fully as possible, the widest range of opinion. At the same time, my own opinions have not been concealed.

Unemployment is not simply an economic problem and it should not be approached in terms of simple economic solutions. The problem extends into all areas of social, personal and moral concern.

Simplistic solutions arising from crude quantitative and theoretical approaches have been advanced repeatedly and have been exposed by events. Clearly the problem of unemployment is qualitative as well as quantitative and it transcends and defies much of modern economic and social analysis.

I am grateful to Macquarie University for extending a Visiting Professorship during the writing of this handbook and to Professor Max Kelly in particular for his assistance. Michael Thompson, Avner Offer and Alan Booth read an earlier version and made many valuable comments and I am grateful to Mrs Sue Macdonald for typing the final draft. I assume full responsibility, of course, for the deficiencies which remain.

Sean Glynn
University of Kent at Canterbury
1989

I

Introduction

'Everyone has the right to work, to free choice of employment . . . and to protection against unemployment.' *United Nations: Universal Declaration of Human Rights, 1948*

'. . . mass, long-term unemployment is the worst breakdown a society can experience, the most damning evidence of political failure.' *Hugo Young, 1987*

'There is no alternative.' *Margaret Thatcher, 1981*

In the early 1980s Britain experienced an economic adversity in which an already high level of unemployment rose dramatically to levels which were unprecedented in the postwar period and only comparable with the 1930s. It became necessary, therefore, to look to history to find comparable British circumstances. There had been serious concern about unemployment in the 1970s and for most of the 1980s unemployment was seen as Britain's leading problem by most commentators, a view confirmed by a long succession of opinion polls. Despite this apparently widespread concern, it was generally agreed that Government was doing little or nothing to tackle the problem directly and many believed that government policies were one of its principal causes.

When Margaret Thatcher became Prime Minister in 1979 unemployment was 1.2 million and falling; by 1983 the total had almost trebled, but the Thatcher Government was returned to office with a greatly increased majority in a General Election dominated by other issues. In earlier decades this political feat would not have been considered possible. Indeed, in 1972 a previous Conservative

Prime Minister embarked on a dramatic reversal of policies – which became known as Heath's U-turn – when it seemed possible that unemployment would reach 1 million. Clearly something changed in the 1980s. In 1987 Mrs Thatcher won a third General Election, in which economic issues loomed large and the fact that unemployment was almost as high as in 1983 did not appear to do the Government significant electoral harm. It appeared that mass unemployment had become politically acceptable at least to a sufficiently large proportion of the electorate to ensure control of Parliament. For a substantial proportion of the population government policies appeared to be working and producing dividends in the form of higher real incomes. There had been some reduction in unemployment, although the total remained very high by previous standards, and this was presented as a sign of success. Sharing a larger national cake amongst a smaller proportion of the population was a magic formula for political success. Meanwhile, sociologists had begun to detect the emergence of an 'underclass' or disadvantaged section of society doomed to poverty and deprivation and economists in analysing the labour market defined 'outsiders' and 'insiders'.[1] Unemployment had a crucial role in creating and conditioning these new economic and social divisions. The massive costs of unemployment in terms of lost production, declining government revenues and increased outlays were given little attention as economists and government colluded in playing down the significance of measured unemployment.

By the mid-1980s it was widely accepted across the political spectrum and internationally that heavy unemployment was inevitable, unavoidable and something which society had to live with.[2] While expressing great concern the British opposition parties made only modest promises about the extent to which they might reduce unemployment. This modesty responded to a sceptical electorate and reflected the views of professional economists and other experts. It was pointed out, time after time, that the world was in economic crisis and that unemployment had risen in many industrial nations, in some to higher levels than in Britain. This plague of unemployment was often presented in crisis terms and it was also frequently suggested that long-term structural and technological influences had destroyed jobs on a large scale and would continue to do so, making unemployment on a massive scale inevitable. There was widespread discussion of 'de-industrialization' and the impact of 'new technology' on 'post-industrial' society.[3] The titles of a series of academic and popular publications reflected these gloomy views about the 'crisis of work' and it was widely assumed that in the 'workless state' most people would have to be educated to cope with much more leisure.[4] In part at least, a dubious futurology served to rationalize the problems of the present. At the same time, there were numerous attempts to minimize concern and to create new views about unemployment. These demonstrated a remarkable range of intellectual ingenuity. It was suggested that many of the unemployed were actually engaged in the so-called informal or 'black' economy, which was estimated to be very substantial. There were also widespread suggestions, encouraged by the Thatcher Government, that many of the unemployed 'did not want work' and that work was available for those who really wanted it. Although this was overwhelmingly disproved by the evidence on employment vacancies, the tendency to blame the victims of unemployment for the problem itself persisted. It was widely assumed, especially by economists, that there was a large voluntary or 'search' element in the unemployed total, much of it induced by generous unemployment and redundancy benefits.[5] There was also a widespread belief that because of welfare and other payments the unemployed did not really suffer as they had in the past. While the unemployment of the 1930s was still regarded as a tragedy, that of the 1980s was not.

These discussions took place against a background of increasingly filthy streets, declining public services, crumbling infrastructure and environmental decay as managers in both the public and the private sectors competed in cutting staff. There was indeed a jobs famine but work which needed to be done remained in unrestricted supply. The ironies of worklessness existing alongside chronic need were largely ignored. One of the most unremarked ironies was in housing where increasing concern about homelessness and soaring prices persisted while house building remained at historically low levels.[6] There had been no diminution in human needs.

In fact there is ample evidence to suggest that full employment is possible as well as desirable and that what is lacking is ends rather than means. Any modern society which desires full employment can achieve it through appropriate organization, although, obviously, other priorities may suffer in the process. The view that present levels of unemployment are inevitable is quite false. During the 1970s British governments ceased to see full employment as a first priority. More recently, unemployment has become the chosen solution in the drive to fulfil certain political, economic and social aims. Britain is one of a small number of nations which have experienced very high levels of unemployment while other industrial countries have managed to escape almost entirely or have experienced significantly lower levels.[7] Some of the influences which create unemployment may operate internationally and some nations may force others into unemployment, but differences between nations clearly indicate that domestic circumstances are more important. Unemployment is not simply the result of economic forces and political, social and cultural influences may be more fundamental.

Governments can influence the level of employment although this is disputed by some economists and politicians.[8] It is important to understand the historical and institutional context in which policy is formulated and implemented. Economic theory cannot explain in adequate and acceptable terms why unemployment has occurred in the past and many of the disputes between adherents of different economic theories must be seen as arcane and irrelevant. It seems to be beyond dispute that economics has no practical short-term solution to the contemporary problem of unemployment. The purpose here is not to attack economics. Indeed, it will be suggested that some understanding of economic theory and its development is essential. However, the fact that some countries have had and still have full employment and that some periods in history have been relatively free of unemployment can only be understood by combining economic theory with historical and empirical study. The

[4]

importance of an historical approach has an additional relevance in the British case in view of the remarkable parallels between the 1980s and the interwar years. Many historians in recent years have experienced a strong sense of *déjà vu* and not least in listening to popular pronouncements about unemployment and economic policy.[9] Comparisons should not be forced, but where they are relevant and real the present is illuminated and we can perhaps learn from experience. The British unemployment experience of the interwar years was the background against which Keynes formulated a revolution in economic thinking while in the early 1980s Britain was a laboratory for monetarism.

The importance of (un)employment

In dealing with unemployment we are also inevitably concerned with employment and the processes which create and destroy jobs. This is sometimes referred to as the 'labour market', a term which is used loosely and may mean a variety of things.[10] If we view unemployment as a stock or absolute number of people without work, the stock may increase or decrease as jobs are created or destroyed, or as people not previously employed seek work. Thus, changes in the level of unemployment result from job gains or losses or changes in the workforce.

In what follows we will be concerned, almost entirely, with regular, paid employment which has assumed a dominant importance in modern industrial society. Informal and unpaid work and the division of labour between the sexes and within the family will not be dealt with, although it is accepted that these activities have considerable social and economic impact. In particular, they may influence the supply of labour in the regular labour market and informal employment may be in part a response to deficiencies in the demand for labour.[11] While new divisions of labour both inside and outside the home have attracted a good deal of new interest in sociological research and discussion, the fact remains that formal employment is overwhelmingly important in terms of income generation and in establishing social position and status. Some attention will be given to new patterns of formal employment including the enhanced importance of paid female labour and self-employment.

In the study and understanding of human beings and human society the importance of employment can hardly be overestimated.[12] It is not only sociology that commences its definition and analysis of society in terms of occupations. The life chances of an individual tend to be heavily influenced by parental occupations which determine social class and many other fundamental influences during the formative years. One's own occupation will probably determine or heavily influence income and wealth, social status and political attitudes, lifestyle, social contacts and much else. In short, the importance of occupations or employment is fundamental both to the individual and society. Through employment we not only derive income or livelihood, we also establish our personal identities and social positions. In order to be integrated into society with a clearly defined role and function most people feel a need to be employed or to have a formal relationship with someone who is. For these reasons employment or the 'right to work' has come to be seen as a basic human right, enshrined in the United Nations Declaration of Human Rights. In the words of E. F. Schumacher, 'useful work, adequately rewarded in some combination of material and non material things, is a central need of human beings, even a basic yearning of the human spirit'.[13]

Emphasizing the importance of employment in modern society helps to make clear the tragedy of unemployment. Unemployment may cause not only loss of income and production, which sooner or later creates poverty and deprivation, but also serious social and psychological problems, many of which are long term and irredeemable. Although the evidence for these problems is now very substantial, the majority who remain in employment often fail to understand the consequences of unemployment. Because the employed tend to value leisure, they may view the unemployed with envy and resentment, especially if the latter do not suffer significant loss of income. These attitudes have not changed over the years and are evident in British society from the late nineteenth century. It must be emphasized, therefore, that voluntary

[6]

unemployment is a rare phenomenon usually associated with social and psychological maladjustment as well as an inability to command rewarding and socially integrating employment.

In its most extreme forms the sense of loss which is experienced by some of those who are denied rewarding employment is equivalent to death – not literally but in social and psychological terms.[14] The unemployed may feel that they have ceased to be active functioning members of society. Unemployment will compel some individuals to accept work which is unsatisfactory in terms of pay or working conditions and society as well as the individual will pay a price for this, perhaps in the form of drunkenness, poverty, child cruelty, wife beating and other familiar problems often associated with inadequate income and stress. These problems may be even worse when there is no form of work available. Thus, unemployment is not simply an economic problem and the problem of unemployment does not simply affect the unemployed. As the distinguished American economist R. M. Solow has suggested, 'the acceptance of lower grade jobs is itself a form of unemployment'.[15] It has been suggested that the non-economic problems associated with unemployment increase as one ascends the social scale.[16] A sacked business executive with a golden handshake may not suffer from loss of income but is more likely to experience stress and social adjustment problems than an unskilled labourer in the same situation. Indeed, the labourer may be glad of a rest and may in some ways be relieved if his job was particularly unpleasant, but he and his family will experience loss of income and may fall into poverty as a result. However, it would be totally wrong to imply that for those who have never had regular, rewarding and well-paid work unemployment is not a tragedy. The truth is that such people have been victims of unemployment all their lives both in and out of work. In looking at unemployment we have to consider the whole labour market including the employed and the pattern of employment.

History indicates that human beings are highly adaptable and are ingenious in coping with adversity.[17] Where the formal economy fails people try to adapt by making other arrangements of an informal kind which often become institutionalized. These will blend with the range of informal and illegal activities which are the result of other influences such as the desire to avoid taxation or safety regulations. Also, unemployment may compel different work patterns within the family where there is no longer dependence on one main (usually male) breadwinner. Casual and part-time work are a traditional response to labour market deficiencies and were common during the nineteenth century.[18] Ironically, during recent years both the so-called 'black economy' and the growth of informal and part-time employment have been advanced as reasons for believing that unemployment does not matter. It must be emphasized, therefore, that there is probably a basic human need for social integration through regular employment and, where this is denied, there will be adverse consequences. Voluntary unemployment was negligible during the 1950s and 1960s and to attribute the sharp rise in unemployment during the 1980s to voluntary factors is manifestly absurd unless one assumes a dramatic change in human nature. Nevertheless, such views are common and much of modern economic theory assumes this.[19] These views will be examined below.

So far the emphasis has been entirely on the negative aspects of unemployment. However, since there has been little evidence of direct government attempts genuinely to reduce unemployment in recent years, or of overwhelming electoral demands that this be done, it seems reasonable to ask if there are positive benefits? What possible gains can be derived from the sufferings of the unemployed, who are drawn, in the main, from the least privileged ranks of society? In order to answer this question it is important to reiterate that unemployment does not simply affect the unemployed. It is rather a conditioning influence on the whole of society as well as being an economic and social barometer indicating the state of the society in which it occurs. Unemployment has been expected to give rise to greater moderation in pay demands where incomes policies have failed. Also, the number of working days lost in strikes may have been reduced by unemployment. There may be more scope for management in promoting more productive work-

[8]

ing arrangements and introducing new technology.[20] The level of unemployment will, in theory at least, influence and reflect what is called the labour market, including the wage bargaining process and the relative power of wage and salary earners and other parties such as employers, consumers and the state. In turn, this will affect the distribution of income and wealth. In deeper terms the level of employment will indicate and influence the employment hopes and life chances of most people. Even those who feel least threatened will not escape the influence since the level of employment is a measure of the degree of choice and the level of job security of the employed. Even for the totally secure there is concern about living in a society with chronic unemployment. Individual security may still be threatened by collective insecurity. We must view both employment and unemployment as a continuum or range of responses to that range of institutionalized possibilities we refer to as 'the labour market'. To see employment and unemployment as distinct entities is valid in some ways but it does tend to hinder an understanding of the social and economic impact of unemployment.

If we remember that unemployment affects everyone it can be seen how it may be used as a mechanism of economic regulation and social discipline and, at the same time, may threaten political stability if it becomes too high. In British history unemployment has tended to work as a de-radicalizing influence, at least in the short run.[21] During the First World War and postwar boom, for example, the Labour Party and the trade unions advanced and militancy reached high levels. With the onset of mass unemployment in 1920 this rapidly ebbed. During the interwar years, against a background of heavy unemployment, there was a long period of Conservative ascendancy and Labour was able to achieve minority rule only for very short periods. In the long run it can be suggested that mass unemployment did fuel demands for radical change, including a commitment to a welfare state and full employment.[22] The 1980s, once again, were a period of Conservative dominance with a weak and divided opposition but heavy unemployment has not, so far, given rise to radical political demands or developments, but instead has weakened both trade unions and the Labour Party. Some would conclude that radical tendencies are more likely to come from the right rather than the left and it may be that right radicalism has been pre-empted by Margaret Thatcher.[23] The political trend after Thatcher will depend very much on the state of the economy, and high levels of unemployment may remain acceptable if prosperity for the majority can be sustained. However, if the economy falters in a serious way a radical reaction seems inevitable.

During the past decade Britain, while continuing to be troubled by some traditional economic problems, has moved towards creating what is widely regarded as a more efficient economy in the narrow economic sense.[24] Major changes in the structure and nature of industrial organization may have taken place and productivity and total output have increased at faster rates than previously. This creation of a more affluent life, probably for the majority, has not been achieved without pain and sacrifice. In the process an economy may have been developed where perhaps 10 per cent or more of the potential workforce is unemployed at peak levels of activity, and many more at other times, and an under-mass of hopeless and underprivileged people created. Unemployment has played a central role in this process and will continue to do so. By the late 1980s Britain provided a leading European example of the 'private affluence, public squalor' syndrome, but the affluence excluded a very large section of the population and public sector squalor and deprivation cast a grim shadow across many private lives. There had been marked increases in crime and a host of other social problems. Filth in the streets and public drunkenness became increasingly common and England became notorious for football hooliganism and riots. Public and social occasions were increasingly marred by drunken, loutish behaviour, itself an expression of personal and social aggression reflecting inadequacy, hopelessness and lack of opportunity. Increasingly sections of the better-off retreated into atomized family units and privatized activities with obvious consequences for collective action, community and social conscience. The collectivist ethos of the 1940s and later decades became increasingly less attractive and the welfare state vision of Britain gradually slipped away. Such a society, even in the inadequate form in which it had existed, could only have been based successfully in a society which enjoyed full employment.

Unemployment is a fundamental influence and manifestation of the economic and social system in which it occurs. Variations in unemployment may influence the nature of society. Even marginal adjustments, whether or not induced by government, will have an economic impact. Heavy unemployment during the interwar years and full employment for three decades after 1940 were important conditioning influences in British history and there can be little doubt that the more recent rise to new levels of unemployment will also have major consequences. This, of course, is fully intended by government. In the political rhetoric of Thatcherism there was frequent reference to 'beating inflation' and curbing the power of trade unions as well as improving efficiency and creating an 'enterprise culture'. Unemployment is undoubtedly a weapon in pursuing these aims although it is unthinkable in modern democratic circumstances actually to admit this. Instead, the Thatcher governments have successfully argued and convinced many that unemployment and other issues of economic and social justice are matters which can only be determined by the 'market' and are not issues for government.[25]

As we shall see, the history of attitudes towards unemployment in Britain is a catalogue of changing perceptions of reality and differing evaluations of possibilities. At the end of the 1930s, even for Keynes, a sustained period with unemployment averaging 5 per cent or less was not conceivable. In fact, for three decades after 1940 the official level did not reach 5 per cent. During the 1970s unemployment levels in excess of 10 per cent were seen as unthinkable and intolerable, but this was reality by 1980 and has remained so for most of the period since. Current views that mass unemployment is here to stay may be equally erroneous and certainly they need to be challenged. Indeed, a sense of history is becoming increasingly relevant after a decade of mass unemployment. Few people under thirty years of age can now recollect an employment situation in which people were, to use a well-known phrase, 'free to choose' and where the urgency of getting almost any job did not override the desire to make a considered choice. In the past decade there has been a massive lowering of social expectations in British society and this has affected the younger generation with particular severity. As a result, few young people can even conceive the possibility that a society which is resolved to do so can ensure full employment. One can only hope that some knowledge of history will engender hope and determination in place of resigned pessimism.

In the following chapter it will be shown that there are major difficulties in defining and measuring unemployment and that in recent years these difficulties have helped to facilitate the downgrading of the unemployment problem. In Chapter III a preliminary attempt is made to establish the basic attitudes of different groups of economists towards the labour market and employment questions in terms of simple economic theories. This is done at the outset in order to inform the understanding of subsequent historical accounts in Chapters III, IV and V. Economic policy is treated separately along with the relationship between policy and theory in Chapter VII. Inevitably an account of unemployment in British history has to give particular attention to the Thatcher Government and this is attempted in Chapter VIII.

II

Measuring Unemployment

'To know how many people are registered as unemployed at any moment is barely a beginning towards knowing anything worth knowing about unemployment.' *William Beveridge, 1931*

'The official definition in use in the UK has been so frequently changed that it is difficult to grasp the underlying trends as they occur. The definition of unemployment is more a question of semantics than of economics. Politicians, like Humpty-Dumpty, can make the word "unemployment" mean what they choose.' *Christopher Johnson, 1988* (author of *Measuring the Economy*, Penguin, 1988)

'The unhappy truth is that this Government doesn't give a fig for facts. It cheerfully fiddles the figures when it can get away with it, as it has done shamelessly with the unemployment statistics; it routinely presents figures selectively or misleadingly; it expects them to support its case rather than stand independently against which the case can be measured; and it thinks nothing of cutting them back in the interests of saving money, which it chooses to call efficiency, thus devaluing language as well as numbers.' *Melanie Phillips, 1989* (*Guardian* correspondent)

Definitions
There are serious problems in defining and measuring unemployment and this has been a controversial matter during the past decade with the Thatcher Government being accused of 'massaging' the figures in order to minimize the official level of recorded unemployment. Many social scientists now believe that the official figures are virtually meaningless.[1]

There is not and never has been a clear and universally accepted definition of unemployment. All definitions are, to some degree, theoretically and socially determined, subjective and arbitrary. Historically unemployment has been defined and measured in many different ways and accurate comparisons over time and between different economies are difficult to make.[2] It follows that all measures of unemployment should be used with caution, scepticism and clear knowledge of what they represent. Long-term and international comparisons should be viewed with even greater reservations.

William Beveridge defined unemployment as being a condition which affected those who were willing and able to work but unable to find it.[3] Although ostensibly very reasonable, this common-sense approach begs many questions. For example, how do we assess the ability and test the willingness? A twelve-year-old boy or a seventy-year-old woman may be able and willing to work, but if they fail to find employment social convention ensures that they cannot be counted as unemployed. Nor can they be counted as part of the workforce although this may be a matter of convention rather than reality. We can be sure that both now and in the past, the unemployment statistics have included some of those who should not have been counted and excluded some of those who should. In other words, unemployment, however defined, has always been measured with some degree of inaccuracy.

Unemployment can be simply defined as *potential* minus *actual* employment, but both of these magnitudes can only be assessed on the basis of arbitrary assumptions about who is and could be employed.[4] In fact, unemployment is usually defined more specifically and measured directly, for example, as those registered for and genuinely seeking work, or claiming benefit as unemployed. In recent years figures quoted for employment have included rising numbers of those who only work part-time, itself a category which cannot be easily defined and measured. Also, several groups, including students, juveniles and men over sixty, have been excluded from the official definition of potential employment (in other words, the workforce). Normally the unemployment statistics are most meaningful when expressed as a percentage of the total workforce.

Measurement

In Britain the statistical record of unemployment reflects the combined influence of subjective definitions and the timing of measurement, but the most important influence has been administrative convenience. In more recent years political and theoretical considerations have also begun to influence the way unemployment is defined and measured.[5]

From the early nineteenth century it is possible to obtain fragmentary information about unemployment from Poor Law records, charities and trade union returns. The first national and official figures were developed by officials of the Board of Trade on the basis of the records of certain trade unions that paid unemployment benefits and kept records of members claiming benefit. These unions were highly atypical as Feinstein suggests:

> the sample is by no means representative: it covers only a limited number of industries . . . only trade unionists . . . mainly skilled workers . . . it does not appear possible to make any statistical assessment of the possible under-or-over-statement involved in the use of the trade union series as a measure of the general unemployment rate.[6]

The official figures based upon trade union returns which can be taken back to 1855 must be viewed with some scepticism as a measure of overall unemployment, if not as a measure of the level of economic activity. This has not prevented many historians and economists from making use of them and taking them at face value. From later and more reliable statistics we know that levels of unemployment amongst skilled workers were much lower than for the workforce as a whole and it is likely, therefore, that the pre-1914 figures give a very misleading impression. To some extent this bias towards skilled workers could be offset by the bias towards export industries which were more susceptible to fluctuations than the domestic economy. We should also note that there are problems in attempting to estimate the workforce and in calculating activity rates and this is an additional reason for urging caution in using pre-1914 unemployment statistics.[7]

It is clear from other evidence that there was a large mass of unskilled labour, particularly evident in London, which was subject to unemployment and underemployment.[8] Also, labour was forced into low productivity activities, such as domestic service, which were unattractive in terms of pay and conditions. According to Treble, the nineteenth-century labour market was 'volatile, highly imperfect, and in certain areas, glutted'.[9] In 1895 Keir Hardie and Will Thorne argued that unemployment affected 1.7 million people.[10] This claim was disputed but the late nineteenth- and early twentieth-century poverty surveys carried out by Booth (London), Rowntree (York), Rathbone (Liverpool), Tawney (Glasgow), Bowley and Burnett-Hurst (Stanley, Northampton, Reading and Warrington) indicated that a quarter to a third of the population lived in some degree of poverty on a rigorous definition. Apart from illness, widowhood and old age, poverty was compatible with employment, as the consequence of low earnings, underemployment and unemployment, all of which were interconnected. Approximately 70 per cent of poverty was attributable, directly, to the deficiencies of the employment situation.[11] What is called the 'labour market' gave rise to a situation whereby labour could not be sold or did not command sufficient reward for widespread poverty to be avoided. These facts should be kept firmly in mind when the official figures are mentioned. These indicate the proportion of trade union members receiving trade union unemployment benefits. They do not reveal other forms of unemployment and, more important, underemployment, and inadequate pay resulting from a lack of employment opportunities.

The official figures for the pre-1914 period suggest that unemployment fluctuated between 2 and 10 per cent over the trade cycle which lasted between seven and eleven years from peak to peak. There were cyclical troughs, for example, in 1878–9, 1884–7, 1892–3, 1904–5, and 1907–9. The average level of unemployment on the official figures between 1855 and 1914 was just under 5 per cent and there is no perceptible change in trend over the period.[12]

With the development of the National Insurance Scheme (NIS) under Part II of the 1911 National Insurance Act and subsequent extensions, alternative unemployment statistics became available as a by-product and these eventually provided the basis for 'official' figures. For most of the interwar period we have NIS returns which covered about 12 million workers, approximately 60 per cent of the workforce, from 1923. Strictly speaking, official NIS statistics date from 1926 since earlier figures based upon the unemployment registers must have included some workers from uninsured trades. The NIS figures were based upon a spot monthly count of those registered on a particular day as being unemployed at Labour Exchanges throughout the UK and this method of counting the unemployed lasted until the early 1980s. Thus from the early 1920s Britain had a method of counting unemployment which was widely accepted by the general public as being accurate and reliable as a measure of unemployment. For the interwar years between 1921 and 1939 the NIS figures suggest an average annual level of unemployment of 14 per cent; a minimum of 10 per cent and a maximum of 23 per cent.[13]

Of course, the NIS figures were far from being a perfect measure and, during the interwar period, both politicians and academics were aware of this.[14] Registration included some people who were not actually seeking work while many of the genuinely unemployed did not register.[15] Indeed, the extent of registration varied directly with the perceived generosity of unemployment benefits. For married women especially there was serious under-recording since they were not usually entitled to benefits in their own right and were disinclined to register where there was little hope of finding employment. Similar considerations applied to young people and to those of pensionable age.[16]

Since they cover only about 60 per cent of the workforce during the interwar period the official or NIS-based employment statistics can be seriously misleading. They clearly understate the absolute numbers of unemployed while overstating the percentage rate of unemployment for the workforce as a whole by 20 per cent or more. The section of the workforce excluded from the NIS was made up of farm labourers (until 1936), domestic servants, the armed forces, civil servants, the self-employed and those earning over £250 per annum. These groups were, on the whole, much less likely to be unemployed than insured workers.[17]

For alternative estimates we have to turn to the census, which, in 1931, successfully recorded and published a census count of unemployment for the first time. Feinstein has compiled an alternative set of unemployment statistics for the interwar years based upon extrapolation from the (revised) 1931 census using NIS figures (also revised) as a base.[18] His workforce figures are based upon Chapman's estimates of man-years of employment.[19] This gives an estimate of annual rates of unemployment for the interwar years which is perhaps comparable with more recent estimates by the Unemployment Unit and various academic groups.[20] Whereas the NIS returns give an annual average of 14.2 per cent for the years 1921–38, Feinstein's estimates indicate an average of 10.9 per cent. Any evaluation of these revised figures must involve some assessment of how typical 1931 was compared with other years in the 1920s and 1930s. There are grounds for suggesting both upward and downward revisions to Feinstein's figures.[21] However, a much more serious problem in using Feinstein's table lies in assessing the value of the 1931 census as a measure of unemployment. Since the Second World War there has been widespread use of census and survey methods of measuring unemployment and these measures continue to be used. The results depend upon the questions asked but as a generalization it may be said that census methods of estimating unemployment, where individuals are simply asked to classify themselves as employed and unemployed, tend to indicate higher levels of unemployment than registration methods.

Many historians regard Feinstein's revised series as the best indication of overall levels and rates of British unemployment in the interwar period. Unfortunately, the series is not comparable with official unemployment figures before, during and since that time. Since the interwar period is often used as a benchmark for discussion of the seriousness of contemporary unemployment, it is worth attempting to make comparisons with official coverage during the post-1945 period when nearly all formal employment in the economy was covered by the NIS. A multiplier of $\frac{8}{13}$ has been suggested in order to adjust interwar NIS figures to approximate comparability with those for the postwar period up to 1982.[22] On this basis the interwar annual average figure of 14.2 per cent becomes 8.7 per cent and this makes unemployment levels in the 1980s seem relatively severe. Using the same basis of comparison, the worst annual figure for the 1930s, 22.1 per cent in 1932, converts to 13.6 per cent. The figure recorded for 1982 was 13.8 per cent and similar levels were recorded during the following four years. Thus it can be said with some degree of confidence that levels of unemployment during the 1980s have tended to be worse than during the interwar period and that the peaks of unemployment during the 1980s have been as bad if not worse than in the worst year of the 1930s. It is also clear from the record that unemployment fell much more rapidly in the 1930s than in the 1980s.

As indicated, NIS coverage was widened after the Second World War to cover almost all formal employment and, with registration as the basis for measuring unemployment, the official figures became *relatively* more accurate in relation to the workforce as a whole. Continuing the interwar practice, the official figures were derived from a count on a particular day each month of those registered as unemployed at employment exchanges. Statistics were released to the press in a monthly statement and subsequently published in the *Department of Employment Gazette*.[23] A count was also made of the 'temporarily stopped' (those laid off work but not actually fired) and, until November 1972, these were included in the official count of unemployment.

With the significant increases in unemployment from 1966 the statistics began to receive new attention and in the early 1970s anti-Keynesians began to question the accuracy of the official measures.[24] The views of new classical economic writers such as Wood, Bourlet and Bell were taken up by Sir Keith Joseph in his Preston speech.[25] These views suggested that governments were being seriously misled by the official statistics which, it was argued, grossly exaggerated the amount of 'involuntary' or Keynesian unemployment. In other words, governments were from time to time expanding money supply in order to combat unemployment which could not be reduced through such techniques. Bourlet and Bell argued that certain groups of unemployed should be excluded from the official figures. These were: school-leavers, frictional or short-term unemployed, 'voluntary unemployed, unemployables, fraudulent unemployed, and convenience unemployed'. These issues were debated by academics and in the financial press.[26] In the 1980s many of these groups were, in fact, excluded from the official count by the Thatcher Government.

Debate about the unemployment statistics continued during the 1970s and by the end of the decade serious doubts about statistics based on registration had been established among officials and academics.[27] Claims about overstatement were balanced by suggestions of understatement in view of the fact that large numbers of those looking for work, and part-time work in particular, were unregistered. Estimates based on census returns and general household surveys confirmed this.[28] The 'discouraged worker' effect, whereby those who saw little prospect of work failed to register, became widely recognized. The Warwick Manpower Research Group estimated that the average propensity to register was 78 per cent for males and only 58 per cent for females – implying an understatement of approximately 30 per cent in the official figures.[29] As a measure of those who would work if work were available at existing wage rates, the registration statistics involved substantial understatement. Thus the official measure of unemployment was attacked on all sides. In the final analysis, the evaluation of the statistics depended very much upon what people wished to measure. The long debate about statistics had an important function in minimizing both expert and public concern over unemployment. In 1983, in an ill-judged post-election editorial, *The Times* appeared to be dismissing 3 million unemployed as 'statistical' rather than real.

Under the Thatcher Government changes in estimating the unemployed became both frequent and controversial and the Government made regular charges that the figures were being made more realistic and that changes were both logical and necessary to bring British statistics into line with those elsewhere. However, almost all the revisions were downwards and this gave credence to accusations of political interference with official measures.[30] This is not the place to review all the changes, which numbered more than twenty, but the important revisions included the following:

In November 1981, the higher long-term rate of supplementary benefit was introduced for men over sixty who had been receiving unemployment benefit for twelve months or more. This cut the official unemployment total by 37,000. In July 1982, unemployment benefits became taxable and in October the part-time list ceased, the latter change reducing official unemployment by 52,000. In October 1982, registration at Job Centres became voluntary and the official unemployment count was based upon *those actually receiving benefit rather than those registered*. It is estimated that this move reduced the official total by 200,000. In June 1983, unemployed men over sixty were allowed long-term supplementary benefit immediately they became unemployed. This cut 54,000 from the official total. Further reductions resulted from the granting of NIS credits to 162,000 men. During the summer months significant reductions in official totals were made by not counting school leavers and university students who registered for work. Also, the self-employed were added to the working population figures and this cut the percentage figures for unemployment by at least one percentage point in 1986/7.

Obviously the official figures were influenced by special training and employment schemes which, by 1986/7 absorbed at least 400,000 people from the benefit list. In 1986 the Unemployment Unit estimated that some 800,000 people were, in fact, unemployed but not registered and that changes in the statistics had reduced the official total by 420,000. An estimate made by Dr Fred Robinson of Newcastle University suggested that the official figures underestimated unemployment by 50 per cent and that the correct total was 4.7 million in March 1987. In a survey of Peterlee new town unemployment was estimated to be 30 per cent, compared with an official figure of 17.6 per cent.[31]

In March 1989, the offical number of unemployed was 1,960,200 or 6.9 per cent of the workforce, but the Unemployment Unit estimated that, without the twenty-five changes the Government had introduced, the total would have been 2,600,000 or 9.1 per cent. As a result of changes in defining and measuring unemployment, the official total had been reduced by about a quarter.[32]

The unemployment statistics completely failed to indicate departures from the workforce in the face of mass unemployment. These included large numbers who were forced into early retirement as well as many of retirement age who would have wished to continue working had work been available: also wives and others who could not find paid employment but were not entitled to benefits. At the same time, the employment totals included many who had been compelled to work part-time when they would have preferred full-time employment and large numbers who had been forced into low-paid and unsatisfactory employment by necessity.

Meanwhile, the official spokesman, Lord Young, was suggesting that the official figures overstated the true level of unemployment and that the annual Labour Force Survey[33] provided a more accurate measure.[34] The latter counted as unemployed only those people who, in the week before being interviewed, were without a paid job and either seeking work, waiting to start a new job or expecting the results of an interview, or prevented from seeking work only by temporary sickness or holiday. By 1987 government representatives were beginning to quote figures compiled by the International Labor Organization (ILO) which counted people without a paid job, available to start work in the next fortnight and who had either looked for work at some time in the previous four weeks or were waiting to start a new job.

Frequent changes in the basis of the official statistics made them unsuitable as a trend indicator. By the mid-1980s the Department of Employment (DoE) had started to re-write history by publishing in the *Gazette* backward projections of the new definitions of unemployment. Statistics were published for earlier years on the new basis, but not for later years on the old basis. Thus in 1986 the average annual level of unemployment in the UK during 1985 was given as 13.5 per cent. By 1989 the *Gazette* had revised this figure downwards to 11.8 per cent. By early 1989 the official percentage figures had fallen below the Labour Force Survey estimates which traditionally had been much lower.

Table 1 (p. 24) attempts to indicate how changes in the method of counting and calculating unemployment had reduced the official figure by spring 1987. Some indication of the possible impact of special measures to reduce unemployment is also given.

In the 1980s the increasing rigour which the authorities sought to apply to the unemployment count bore comparison with the interwar 'not genuinely seeking work' exclusions from benefit.[35] By the middle of the decade a bewildering array of statistics relating to employment and unemployment were being produced and the issue of measurement had become both political and confused. Frequent revisions in the official statistics made them unsuitable for comparative purposes, including academic research, and increasingly meaningless. On the one hand an increasing number of commentators drew attention to the question of 'hidden unemployment' and 'discouraged workers' while the Government's spokesmen also deprecated the official statistics by suggesting that many of those included were not actually seeking employment. There was also debate about employment growth which depended in turn upon what was counted and over what period growth (or decline) was measured. Increasingly, as the 1980s continued, there were government attempts to measure from 1983, the nadir, rather than the 1979 peak. These arguments seem to have fooled many experts as well as a bewildered general public.

While it is important to attempt to measure unemployment it is clear that we should not set too much store by any particular set of figures. Unemployment is a social and qualitative rather than a quantitative phenomenon and it cannot be measured with great precision. This is clearly illustrated by the historical comparisons which have been made and which reveal that unemployment, as well as the methods of enumerating it, has changed over time and that the arbitrary line drawn between the employed and the unemployed may not be so meaningful as is often supposed. It may be said that in attempting to assess the unemployment problem we are really seeking to evaluate employment conditions and prospects

Table 1 *Main Changes in Methods of Measuring Unemployment 1979–89 (000s)*

Date	Change	Estimated effect
October 1979	Fortnightly payment of benefits	+ 20
November 1981	High long-term rate of supplementary benefit for men over sixty on unemployment benefit twelve months or more	−37
July 1982	Benefits became taxable	?
October 1982	Ending of part-time list	−52
October 1982	Registration at Job Centres made voluntary. Computer count of benefit claimants replaces count of those registered	−190
March 1983	Unemployed men over sixty taken off unemployment benefit	−162
July 1985	Correction of N. Ireland discrepancies	−5
March 1986	Two-week delay in compilation of figures to reduce over-recording	−50
	Total	−476
Total estimated effect, seasonally adjusted, April 1987		−510

Also, school leavers plus university students registered not counted

July 1986	Inclusion of self-employed and HM forces in denominator of unemployment percentage. Reduced unemployment per cent by	1.4

Effect of special measures in reducing unemployment (March 1987)

1 Job creation	Community Programme	220
	New Workers' Scheme	6
	Enterprise Allowance Scheme	15
2 Other measures	Job Release Scheme	23
	Availability-for-work test	6
	Restart Scheme	104
	Benefit changes	15
3 Training schemes	Job Training Schemes	0*
	Youth Training Scheme	0*
Total		389

*It is impossible to estimate the effects of these schemes on the unemployment count.
Source: C. Johnson, *Measuring the Economy* (1988), Tables 20, 21.

in qualitative terms. Unemployment statistics, handled with great care, can certainly assist in this but in themselves they are little more than a starting point.

Variations in unemployment
Although the discussion of unemployment statistics has focused on aggregates, and annual aggregates at that, it must be emphasized that these may conceal more than they reveal. Disaggregation is essential. Many writers have emphasized that unemployment should be viewed as a flow rather than a stock and it is important to examine variations in terms of region, duration, age, sex, social class, industry, occupation and other dimensions. Space does not permit a full discussion of variations in unemployment along the above lines but a few brief comments can be made.[36]

Regional dimensions have always been a major feature of British unemployment and this has been an important influence on attitudes. Before 1914 the industrial and relatively prosperous areas of the midlands, the north, Wales and Scotland were not thought to have serious unemployment problems. However, they were affected by cyclical unemployment and slumps which, during the late nineteenth century, came every 7–11 years. During these periods of depression trade union statistics recorded unemployment levels of about 10 per cent. In the less industrial areas before 1914 there were chronic problems of underemployment, low pay and casual labour systems. These problems may have been especially severe in London and in east London in particular where the docks relied heavily on casual hiring.[37]

After 1914 the regional pattern began to change.[38] A more regularized pattern of employment began to emerge in the less industrialized areas and in the interwar years from 1921 the most highly industrialized areas with heavy concentrations of 'old staple' industries emerged as the unemployment black spots with heavy unemployment persisting over the cycle at well above the national average. Some writers have seen this as a reversal of the pre-1914 situation whereby the once relatively rich industrial areas, which had pioneered the Industrial Revolution and helped to make Britain the 'workshop of the world', became relatively poor and depressed. In the interwar years the coalfield areas of south Wales, Lancashire, Yorkshire, the north-east and central Scotland became synonymous with unemployment. Meanwhile, in the south, and especially the south-east, there was relative prosperity and much lower levels of unemployment. In June 1936, unemployment varied from 32 per cent in Wales to 17 per cent in Scotland and north-west England, to 5 per cent in the south-east on the official (NIS) figures.[39]

During postwar full employment regional problems remained and there were major differentials which echoed those of the interwar years, although the absolute levels of unemployment recorded were usually much lower. Northern Ireland continued to experience the highest levels of unemployment in the UK. Regional disparities continued and intensified with the rise in unemployment from the 1970s and the phasing out of British regional policies in the 1980s although there was some compensation from EEC sources. With the re-emergence of mass unemployment in the 1980s there were obvious comparisons with the interwar years. Unemployment struck most savagely in manufacturing industries in the old industrial areas. However, by the 1980s the employment pattern was less specialized on a regional basis and service occupations were relatively more important. As a result, regional differentials were not so acute as in the years between the wars. In 1987 the official figure for unemployment in the south-east was 6.5 per cent. London, East Anglia, the south-west and the east midlands had slightly higher levels but were all well below the national average of 10.67 per cent (official). The remainder of Britain had levels which were above the national average and approximately double the figure for the south-east. Northern Ireland, with unemployment at 17.5 per cent, was well above any other region of the UK.[40]

The duration of unemployment is an area of study in its own right and in recent years the 'long-term unemployed' have been given particular attention by academic writers and by government.[41] Long-term unemployment is usually defined, quite arbitrarily, as unemployment lasting for one year or more. Clearly the poverty associated with unemployment is likely to increase with duration and will probably be concentrated among the long-term unemployed. The same applies, of course, to most of the other forms of damage, material and non-material, which may arise from unemployment. It has frequently been pointed out that after long periods of being without work people may become apathetic and demoralized and several studies during the 1930s pointed this out. In 1930–1 researchers at Warsaw University compiled biographies of fifty-seven unemployed men. At about the same time there was an intensive study of unemployment in Marienthal, a small industrial town near Vienna which was blighted by factory closure.[42] On the basis of these studies, Eisenberg and Lazarsfeld developed a stage theory of unemployment which has had many echoes. They concluded:

'First there is shock, which is followed by an active hunt for a job, during which the individual is still optimistic and unre-signed . . . Second, when all efforts fail, the individual becomes pessimistic, anxious and suffers active distress; this is the most crucial stage of all. And third, the individual becomes fatalistic and adapts himself to his new state but with a narrower scope. He now has a broken attitude.'[43]

In Britain the Warsaw biographies may have helped to inspire *Memoirs of the Unemployed* by Beales and Lambert and there have been many other intensive studies of long-term unemployment.[44] More recently Richard Layard and other economists have indicated that the long-term unemployed may, in effect, have left the labour market, either because they are no longer physically or mentally fit for work or because employers may prefer those who have been out of work for shorter periods.[45] The possibility of becoming trapped in long-term unemployment is well documented. These findings have helped to give rise to special measures to deal with the long-term unemployed and they are increasingly treated as a separate category.

In the 1920s long-term unemployment, on the usual twelve-month definition, was a relatively small part of the unemployment total at 7–12 per cent. However, in the early 1930s there was a sharp increase and the proportion stuck at around 25 per cent and persisted until the end of the 1930s.[46] It is clear that a sharp increase in the general level of unemployment will escalate long-term unemployment and that this may persist for long periods even though aggregate unemployment is falling. This was brought out by the experience of the 1980s when long-term unemployment came to exceed the 1930s proportion rising from 14 per cent of the official unemployed total in 1975 to 40 per cent by 1984 in spite of a complex series of special measures aimed at those out of work for long periods.[47]

During the 1980s it is clear that age has had a crucial bearing on the incidence of unemployment. The most severe problems have affected the over-forties and the under-twenty-fives and teenage unemployment, because of its chronic dimensions, has become a topic of particular attention. Older workers were not necessarily more likely to become unemployed since decreased physical capacity is more than offset by greater experience, skill and reliability. Also, last-in-first-out rules favoured age. However, older men who had the misfortune to become unemployed often found it harder to find fresh employment.

Youth unemployment in the 1970s and 1980s was largely a reflection of the difficulty of entering an oversupplied workforce in which many employers were simply not interested in training or recruiting.[48] Also, the products of high birth rates during the 1960s were attempting to enter the labour market, although this demographic increase varied in its impact. Despite the similarity of circumstances during the interwar years there does not appear to have been a comparable youth unemployment problem despite earlier school leaving. Youth unemployment between 1920 and 1939 averaged only 5 per cent against an overall average of 14 per cent (NIS). Possibly this can be explained by under-recording in the official statistics, but it has also been suggested that, in the absence of unemployment benefits, young people priced themselves into work by accepting much lower wages, relative to the national average, than teenagers earn today.[49] Eichengreen has also stressed demographic factors (a lower ratio of juveniles to adults than now), the composition of employment (which was more biased towards industries employing a high proportion of young people) and less emphasis on seniority.[50]

In 1986, unemployment for those in the first year after school was running at 30 per cent and was over 50 per cent in many areas despite an economic growth rate of over 3 per cent.[51] This suggested that youth unemployment would continue to be a serious problem. Nevertheless, unemployment benefits for sixteen and seventeen year-olds were abolished in 1988 which, in effect meant that unemployment for this age group was not officially recognized. Quite clearly, youth unemployment on such a massive scale had disturbing connotations for the future of society, in terms of its relationship to crime and other social problems, as well as the economy. In London in 1988/9 the emergence of what became known as 'Cardboard City', a settlement of mainly young people sleeping 'rough' near the Festival Hall, served to highlight the plight of the young, unemployed and homeless. Britain's future as an industrial nation could only be based upon an adequately trained and motivated workforce. Unfortunately, education had been sold to the masses not for its own sake but as a route to higher incomes. With heavy unemployment this now seemed questionable.[52] Ironically, the emergence of the most chronic, mass, youth unemployment problem in history did not lead to a questioning of national economic management so much as an attack upon the educational system and upon the poor quality of young people it was accused of producing. Armed with this dubious rationale for 'education reform', Sir Keith Joseph and later Kenneth Baker introduced education cuts and reorganization which antagonized and demoralized the teaching professions and denied university places to large numbers of home students who were potentially capable of taking advantage of them.

As indicated, the official statistics for the interwar years suggest that youth unemployment was below the average for the workforce as a whole. In the 1960s it appeared to be much the same as the overall average. The youth unemployment problem which emerged in the 1970s was so alarming that special measures were rapidly

[29]

introduced. The Youth Opportunities Scheme of 1977 eventually became the Youth Training Scheme of 1983. By that time over half of eighteen-year-olds were either unemployed or on special schemes. In 1981 riots had taken place in several British cities and youth unemployment was seen as a contributing factor.[53] Since most crimes were committed by young men under the age of twenty-five it seemed doubly unfortunate that unemployment should strike this age group so severely. Positive links were established between unemployment and imprisonment,[54] suicide,[55] and a range of social problems. Youth was especially vulnerable and those who suffered a blighted youth could face lifelong problems for which society would pay a price. In economic terms there were also very serious grounds for concern with talk of a 'collapse of training' and the danger of chronic skill shortages when the economy revived. This was certainly the case in the boom of 1988/9 which coincided with a reduced supply of young people for demographic reasons. As the economy turned downwards in 1989 demographic trends remained the main grounds for hoping for some improvement.

It is not surprising, therefore, that the Thatcher Government treated youth unemployment as an emergency and opted for massive intervention. It was simply too important to be left to the market. The massive extension of the Youth Training Scheme (YTS) and related schemes reduced recorded unemployment and provided a new source of cheap labour for employers. By the later 1980s it was being suggested that the YTS was 'an apprenticeship into working class adulthood and higher education an apprenticeship into middle class life'.[56] Meanwhile, traditional industrial apprenticeship had been largely eliminated without the introduction of any viable alternative. After more than a decade of chronic youth unemployment there had been a marked relative fall in the earnings of young people. They, above all, had suffered a dramatic adjustment in expectations.

Differences in the sexual impact of unemployment have been and remain something of a mystery because of inadequate recording of female unemployment. NIS and benefits statistics usually indicate that more men than women are affected. Male unemployment rose from 2 per cent in the 1950s to 17 per cent in 1985, but there is no consistent series for women. In the 1980s about 70 per cent of recorded unemployment was male.[57] But it is well known that, both in the interwar years and since, many unemployed women have been 'discouraged' from the registers and also, of course, married women do not always qualify for benefit in their own right when unemployed. Although much sexual discrimination against women remains in employment there is no doubt that married women have made important advances since the 1930s. Nowadays they are less likely to be victimized where redundancies have to be made and may have more chances than men of finding new employment if they become unemployed. Assumptions that married women should be 'first out' or should not be working at all were very common during the interwar years. Since 1950 the most dramatic change in the British employment pattern has been in the entry of large numbers of married women into paid employment although this is frequently part-time. While many women find part-time employment convenient, some have been compelled to accept it in lieu of full-time work. Unemployment has encouraged the creation of part-time jobs by employers who are well aware of the advantages, to them, of part-time employment. It is insufficiently recognized that part-time workers have very limited rights in employment under existing legislation, that they are difficult to organize and suffer low pay and poor conditions of employment.

Unemployment always has a pronounced social class dimension and its impact tends to increase down the social scale. This was clearly illustrated during the 1930s by Colin Clark who pointed out that manual workers were seven times more likely to be unemployed than professional workers.[58] Writing of unemployment in the 1980s Bean, Layard and Nickell comment that 'unemployment is basically a matter affecting manual workers and low-skilled non-manual workers such as shop assistants'.[59] Clearly this is also reflected in the occupational structure of unemployment. Although 'managerial' and white-collar unemployment has attracted some attention in recent years the fact remains that the

[31]

problem in both numerical and relative terms remains overwhelmingly manual.[60]

Unemployment has an industrial and occupational dimension in that workers in some industries and with certain skills are more likely to become unemployed. Between the wars there is no doubt that a high proportion of the unemployed had previously been employed in the old staple industries, including coal, cotton, shipbuilding, iron and steel, mechanical engineering. In 1914 these accounted directly for a quarter of total employment. They expanded during the war and postwar boom and then declined sharply in the early 1920s losing at least a million jobs. In the 1920s a high proportion of the unemployed had previously worked in the old staples. As late as 1929 they accounted for half of insured unemployment.[61] In the 1980s the unemployment pattern was more complex but manufacturing industry accounted for the major part of the job loss. Of course, much of unemployment does not arise from redundancy. Also, previous employment is only an approximate guide to the changing structure of the economy.

It will be clear from the above comment that the pattern of employment is extremely complex and that, given the problems of definition and measurement, all generalizations must be made with a great deal of caution. Research into various aspects of the problem has snowballed in recent years and an enormous volume of literature has been published and there is no doubt that this will continue. In a short work of this kind it is impossible to review or even to summarize this literature adequately but an attempt has been made to present the main findings. We now turn to an examination of theories relating to unemployment.

III

Understanding Unemployment

'The ideas of economists and political philosophers are more powerful than is commonly understood. Indeed the world is ruled by little else. Political men, who believe themselves to be quite exempt from any intellectual influence, are usually the slave of some defunct economist.'   *J. M. Keynes, 1936*

'The drastic change that has occurred in economic theory has not been the result of ideological warfare . . . it has responded almost entirely to the force of events.'   *Milton Friedman, 1977*

The intention in this chapter is to indicate, very briefly and in broad outline, how economists have reacted to unemployment problems, in both empirical and theoretical terms, since the 1880s. During that period it may be said that there has been a consistent attempt to assert the notion of a functioning 'labour market', but this has given rise to theories which have often appeared to conflict with rather than to explain reality. The term 'unemployment' first began to be used in its modern sense in the 1880s and appeared in the *Oxford English Dictionary* in 1895.[1] By this time most economists had begun to give serious attention to what was seen as the problem of unemployment.

Types of unemployment
During the past century economists and empirical observers have attempted to distinguish and classify different types of unemployment. One of the first recorded typologies was that produced by Llewellyn-Smith, of the Labour Department of the Board of Trade, in 1886.[2] All attempts to identify particular types of unemployment are based upon concepts of causation. Since there are many different

causes it is possible to distinguish many different types of unemployment.

With the recognition of an unemployment problem in Britain from the 1880s empirical observers began to classify unemployment according to its perceived causes. Beveridge, through his involvement with Toynbee Hall in east London, was one of a number of influential figures who recognized a problem of underemployment which was linked with casual labour systems. Industries which made use of casual labour, such as the London docks, tended to attract a workforce they could only employ when operating at peak capacity. As a result, they generated *casual* unemployment. Beveridge and other reformers tended to assume that the poverty and distress which appeared to result from casual hiring could be eliminated by regulating and regularizing employment. The truth was that such systems were the consequence of an oversupplied labour market and a symptom, therefore, of unemployment and the absence of any adequate system of employment or unemployment relief. By the 1960s, in a very different labour market, casual hiring had almost disappeared. Employment situations ranged from enforced idleness through varying degrees of casual, informal and part-time employment to the regular ten-hour day of the 'labour aristocracy'.

At most times in modern history certain people have been classified as 'unemployable'. This is a term which should be used with more caution than is traditional. In a sense, all the involuntary unemployed are 'unemployable' and could be so classified at any point in time. At the other extreme, during periods of acute labour scarcity, almost all people in the community have been able to perform useful services when called upon and assisted to do so. This was the case during the Second World War when only those with severe physical and mental handicap failed to be integrated into the employment structure. In more recent years much has been done by organizations representing the physically handicapped to make employers aware that far more disabled people can be employed in ways which reward society as well as themselves. Similar developments have commenced with the mentally handicapped but these have further to go. What is termed unemployability is determined in large part by social attitudes and through the social provision (or lack) of education and other facilities. It is clearly in the social interest to make as many people as possible employable but this is much more difficult when there is general unemployment.

Economists have long recognized that regular natural variation, usually climatic, may affect employment and cause *seasonal* unemployment. Stedman Jones details how in late nineteenth-century London large sections of unskilled labour in particular were subject to irregular employment on a seasonal pattern which affected income, population mobility and the division of labour in the family.[3] Seasonal unemployment was not confined to traditional industries. There were marked seasonal fluctuations, for example, in the rapidly developing motor industry during the interwar years and many modern industries such as tourism are similarly affected.

At any point in time a small proportion of workers in the economy will, for various reasons, be between jobs and this is referred to as *frictional* unemployment. Obviously, this type makes up a large part of the 'irreducible minimum' of unemployment which will occur even in an overheated economy. It also features heavily in the 'natural rate' which is discussed below. Hughes and Perlman indicate that 'It is the unemployment arising from a lack of instantaneous adjustment of supply to demand, caused by imperfections in knowledge and mobility, that is called frictional unemployment.'[4]

From the Middle Ages onwards it is possible to find examples of workers being displaced by the introduction of new techniques and this is sometimes labelled *technological* unemployment. As always, economists see this as yet another example of market 'imperfection' whereby workers displaced from one industry cannot be readily absorbed by another. An early modern English cloth maker impoverished by the New Draperies may have viewed the problem in rather less mechanistic terms. Workers are human beings and, in the real world, they are not uniform interchangeable units of production; those displaced by one industry may be useless to another. Both jobs and workers are heterogeneous. In recent years, most types of unemployment which arise from what can be labelled 'market supply–demand mismatches' have been referred to as *structural* unemployment which is usually seen as a longer-run, supply-side problem. In fact, structural unemployment may arise from both supply and demand-side influences. Changing industrial techniques, location or consumer tastes may generate unemployment which has structural characteristics. The classic example of structural unemployment in British history resulted from the decline of the 'old staple' industries during the interwar period. As a result, there was chronic unemployment in the old industrial areas while new and growing industries were located elsewhere. During the interwar years, between 1920 and 1939, the level of NIS unemployment in Britain never fell below 10 per cent and a large part of this problem was structural unemployment, linked either directly or indirectly to the declining industries.[5] In the 1980s again a structural problem has been perceived in that a high proportion of unemployment is male and centred in manufacturing industry which is experiencing exporting difficulties or technological obsolescence.

During the interwar years there were two major peaks of unemployment in 1921 and 1929–32 and it is commonly agreed that one of the main influences here was *cyclical*. As the term implies, cyclical unemployment results from downturns in economic activity associated with business or trade cycles. Cyclical unemployment is normally assumed to result from decisions to postpone investment and/or consumption and is the result, therefore, of a deficiency of demand and essentially a short-term problem. Although economists have given a great deal of attention to fluctuations in the level of economic activity, and several different kinds of cycle have been defined, there is no generally accepted theory or real empirically based understanding of trade cycles. During the late nineteenth century a regular trade cycle pattern was discerned with the so-called 'classic' trade cycle lasting, on average, about nine years from peak to peak. However, many historians consider that the classic cycle was a myth. The fluctuations which gave rise to periodic peaks in unemployment were the result of interacting long swings in economic activities such as building rather than a trade cycle as such. Also, there is no generally accepted explanation of the world depression which commenced in 1929 with the Wall Street Crash. Keynesians and monetarists have different approaches with the former placing the emphasis on demand deficiencies and the latter stressing money supply.[6] Cyclical unemployment certainly appears to exist, but there are difficulties in explaining and predicting its occurrence.

The types of unemployment mentioned so far cannot, in the final analysis, be clearly distinguished from each other and people who are unemployed may fall under more than one heading. Also, different types of unemployment tend to reinforce and react upon each other so that, for example, during a cyclical downturn most types of unemployment will tend to increase. The types distinguished so far are essentially descriptive labels which reflect views about the causes of and remedies to unemployment but lack clear definition and analytical validity. However, descriptive labels can be useful and there is no doubt that new types of unemployment will be defined in the future. One recent example is 'convenience' unemployment, the term used to describe retired people under sixty-five who register as unemployed in order to acquire NIS credits. Possibly, in the near future terms will be invented to describe people who become unemployed as a result of company takeovers or cuts in public expenditure.

If we examine economic discussion about unemployment in recent years it is possible to suggest as a simplification that there have been basically three approaches by economists to employment questions: these can be termed classical, Keynesian and new micro-economic (sometimes called monetarist or neo-classical or new classical). Since the first and the third of these have important similarities they can be combined into a 'classical' view and attitudes to unemployment can be divided into two kinds – Keynesian and classical. The former approach stresses demand deficiency and the latter usually argues in terms of supply-side constraints or market failure. Unfortunately, the issue is complicated by the fact that all unemployment is, in a sense, the result of demand deficiency while, at the same time, it can also be attributed to market failure.

The classical view

The classical view was developed by British economists during the eighteenth and nineteenth centuries and it continued to dominate academic economic thinking until the Second World War. The central feature of classical economic thinking was the idea of a 'market mechanism' which was first developed by Adam Smith in his *Wealth of Nations* (1776). Smith argued that if individuals followed their own interests an 'invisible hand' would regulate a most efficient outcome, which would be in the general interest. Competition would ensure efficiency and a maximization of income and wealth. Thus Smith advocated an absence of government regulation and interference beyond certain basic functions such as defence, law and order, the provision of education, protection of the poor, and the elimination of monopolies and restrictive practices which interfered with perfect competition. This idea is without any doubt the most powerful notion in the history of economics.[7]

Classical economics took the view that the free market would promote full employment and that this was the normal condition. Any unemployment which occurred must either be voluntary or due to 'interference' with the market, which would solve involuntary unemployment problems automatically if left to its own devices. Invariably, unemployment was attributed to 'wage rigidity', that is to wages being too high. The classical view rested upon Say's Law, which stated that supply created its own demand so that underconsumption or overproduction could not occur. Say's Law had been developed from the idea that the income generated in producing goods and services in the economy created an equal amount of demand for goods and services. As a result, a *general* deficiency of demand was impossible in a free market, although individual sectors could experience unemployment. By the end of the century this had been augmented by the average wage-marginal product identity. The latter can be expressed in the form of a simple diagram (Figure 1). According to the theory of diminishing returns,

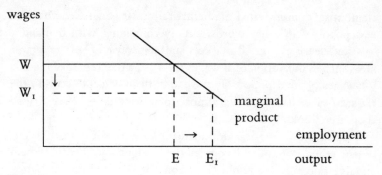

Figure 1

adding extra units of labour, with other factors of production held constant, will eventually lead to progessively smaller additions to output. In other words, the marginal product of labour (the extra output produced by the last person engaged) will eventually start to diminish as employment is expanded. For this reason the marginal product line in the diagram slopes downwards. Employers will expand employment to the point where wage equals marginal product. So, in our diagram, if the wage is W, employment will be E. Where employment is less than E extra workers produce more in extra product than they are paid in wages and it will therefore pay to employ more. Where employment is greater than E the wage will be higher than marginal product and the employer will make a loss if employment is expanded to this point. In effect, therefore, the marginal product curve is the demand curve for labour. If the price of labour, in other words the wage, is set then the level of employment follows automatically. Only a change in wages or productivity can change the level of employment. If we assume that labour is not fully employed at E, but could be so at E_1, this can be achieved by a reduction in wages from W to W_1. An increase in wages above W would reduce employment.

These very simple and abstract ideas help to illustrate the essence of the classical view of the labour market. This was established during the early decades of the nineteenth century and refined by the later development of marginal analysis. L. Walras, the Belgian economist, demonstrated mathematically that general equilibrium was possible (in other words, supply coinciding with demand – 'market clearing' – in all markets simultaneously). Less reputable ideas such as the notion of a 'wages fund', or a fixed share of income for wages, were dropped. By the end of the nineteenth century the classical view had achieved almost total domination over British economic thinking.

Despite the theoretical dominance of the classical view, economists could not fail to recognize the existence of unemployment and its emergence as a public issue from the 1880s. Many, including Alfred Marshall, accepted that the labour market was different from product markets in general; not least because it applied to human beings and involved ethical and other non-economic considerations. While the pure theory remained largely unaltered, an increasing number of economists and other informed observers came to favour intervention, on practical and humanitarian ground, in order to ease unemployment problems.[8]

In the 1860s Karl Marx had argued that capitalism depended upon the creation of a 'reserve army' of unemployed workers. The function of this reserve was to depress wages and enhance profits or 'surplus value'. From time to time capitalism would enter crises where the survival of the system depended upon large-scale creation of unemployment: 'The whole form of movement of modern industry depends, therefore, upon the constant transformation of a part of the labouring population into unemployed or half employed hands.'[9] Although Marxian theory did not find general favour among the English intelligentsia, the view that unemployment was endemic to the capitalist system persisted on the basis of simple observation. In 1886 the economist Foxwell argued that 'uncertainty of employment is the root evil of the present industrial regime'.[10] Charles Booth estimated, after his survey of poverty in London, that 11.5 per cent of workers in east London were 'chronically superfluous' and concluded 'our modern system of industry will not work without some unemployed margin'.[11] Above all there was concern about casual and cyclical unemployment and growing support for public works as a temporary means of relief.

The most sustained attempt to create an alternative to the classical view came from J. A. Hobson. He was the first economist to define unemployment as involuntary idleness for whatever economic reason. Hobson challenged the Board of Trade statistics on unemployment and accused them of understating the problem. In his 'long and persistent career as an economic heretic'[12] Hobson stressed underconsumption and lack of effective economic demand as the cause of unemployment. In *The Problem of Unemployment* (1896) he proposed income redistribution and increasing state intervention and continued to reiterate these views over a long period. Hobson's arguments gained little support in the period before the First World War because his theoretical analysis was unacceptable to the mainstream of professional economics and his broader proposals lacked moral or ideological support. In asserting the idea of 'underconsumption' Hobson was attacking Say's Law which had become a basic article of faith in British classical economics. The rejection of underconsumption by a long line of mainstream economists and writers on economic affairs has been described by T. W. Hutchison as 'the most successful and important campaign of intellectual aggression and terminological dogmatism in the history of economic thought'.[13] Hobson was prevented from pursuing a successful academic career. More recently he has been seen as a 'proto-Keynesian' and, after 1914, an important influence behind the economic programme of the British Labour Party.

During the interwar period the classical view that unemployment was a temporary aberration became increasingly untenable as massive unemployment persisted. Either the classical theory was wrong or it did not apply to the real world. Keynes appears to have commenced with the latter view before moving towards a partial and not wholly successful attempt to establish the former.

The average wage–marginal product identity was and is perfectly logical in terms of its own restrictive assumptions which include perfect competition and constant returns to scale. In the real world most of these assumptions did not and do not apply. Nevertheless, during the interwar years, and again during the 1980s, economists and politicians have assumed that there is a simple trade-off between wages and employment and have argued that lower wages create employment. Certainly, during the interwar period there appears to have been a failure of the market mechanism in the sense that wages failed to adjust (i.e. fall) during a time of prolonged and heavy unemployment. The same phenomenon has been repeated during the 1980s when real wages have risen sharply in the face of mass unemployment. Many economists see this failure of wage adjustment as the main cause of unemployment in both periods.

In the decades before 1914 the British wage structure appears to have been relatively flexible and during times of rising unemployment there were usually general wage reductions. Such reductions were unpopular and resisted, sometimes successfully. Also, wage relativities were remarkably rigid and appear to have been strictly enforced – even in the absence of trade unions. Indeed, the wage structure pre-dated the widespread establishment of unions. During economic downturns employers were able, to some extent, to cut costs and protect profitability by reducing wages. The alternative was, of course, to shed labour and this also happened. From the 1920s there was increasing reliance on the latter rather than the former. Over time, wage flexibility appears to have diminished although this may have occurred rather later in Britain than in other industrial nations.[14] In the early 1920s there were sharp wage reductions, sometimes on the basis of agreed sliding scales, but after that general downward adjustments in nominal wage rates appear to have ceased. Classical theory of the labour market was based upon the belief that a fall in the demand for labour would cause wages to fall until employment levels were restored. This has simply not happened in Britain since the 1920s. During periods of adversity employers came to rely more on workforce reductions and less on wage flexibility. From the early 1920s money wages, on average, remained approximately constant at £3 per week until 1940 while prices fell about 15 per cent. Thus, real wages were tending to increase through the interwar years despite heavy unemployment and industrial decline. In the 1980s money wages have kept well ahead of inflation and real wages have increased strongly. During much of the 1980s the rate of growth in money wages was double the rate of inflation. This failure of wages to adjust in the classical manner is often attributed to trade union strength. However, this can at best be only a partial explanation. Non-unionized workers also experienced real wage increases and the sharp rise in both periods took place despite what appeared to be much weaker union movements.[15]

Real wages depend upon price levels as well as money earnings and during the 1930s and the 1980s the terms of trade moved strongly in Britain's favour. Falling commodity prices in both periods explain much of the improvement in real wages. However, this does not account for the maintenance of money wages against falling prices during the interwar years and the much stronger increase in wages than prices in the 1980s. In both periods employers failed to enforce wage reductions although encouraged to do so by government. In part wage costs may have been offset by rising productivity and reductions in non-wage costs so that profits were maintained in the interwar years and greatly enhanced in the 1980s. In these circumstances, employers had to have very special reasons for a frontal assault on the wages of existing employees; not least because this would run the risk of damaging productivity performance and future recruitment. But the main point appears to be that there was, as Keynes correctly perceived, a fundamental change in the labour market after the First World War. The last major adjustment in wages in the British economy appears to have taken place in 1921–2 after the collapse of the postwar boom. From this point onwards the labour market ceased to operate in the classical manner although many economists continued to believe, or to wish, that it could and would do so. This change coincided with the establishment of a comprehensive system of unemployment benefit which covered almost the entire workforce from the mid-1920s. From this time most workers who experienced unemployment had access either to NIS or the dole in some form. Only a very small minority were forced to resort to the Poor Law in destitution. Although unemployment benefit during the interwar years was far from generous, it was sufficient to condition the labour market. Interwar poverty surveys indicate that those living on the Dole alone were below the least generous poverty line.[16] However, it was enough to prevent a general shattering of wage rates as the result of desperation. It also eliminated much of the underemployment, casual and part-time features of the pre-1914 years, which was based on desperation, and domestic service also declined. Of course, the establishment of a system of unemployment benefits reflected social and political developments. In the absence of unemployment relief wages might have adjusted but the risks in social and political terms were too great to be contemplated.[17]

The Keynesian view

John Maynard Keynes commenced his reassessment of economic theory with the observation that wages in the modern economy were not flexible downwards and, in any case, wage reductions would not necessarily solve unemployment problems. The Keynesian explanation of unemployment relied heavily upon the notion of demand deficiency. In a situation of 'Keynesian unemployment' producers cannot sell product which it would be profitable to produce at existing prices and wages. There is, therefore, a quantity constraint imposed by lack of market demand. Lower wages cannot help and producers can only respond by reducing output and employment below the optimum level. In these circumstances cutting wages would cut demand still further. Keynes argued that there was no reason why the economy should stabilize at the full employment level and indeed that it might settle at much lower levels.

According to Keynes, the levels of output and employment were determined by *aggregate demand*. This is usually expressed in the simple Keynesian formula:

$$Y = C + I + G$$

where Y equals national income or expenditure (aggregate demand), C is consumption, I is investment and G is government spending. Since wages were not flexible downwards it followed that aggregate demand should be increased until employment was raised to an acceptable level. This involved raising *C*, *I* or *G* individually or in combination. The appropriate measures to raise the level of employment were budget deficits, tax reductions, increased govern- ment spending, especially on public works and other employment generating activities. It was also possible that private investment could be stimulated through a reduction in interest rates.

The Keynesian view failed to win broad support or significantly influence policy until the 1940s but it dominated economic thinking for the following three decades. By the 1970s Keynesian views were beginning to experience the same fate as classical views in the interwar years – they appeared not to explain reality. By the 1970s two generations of graduate economists who had been taught that there was a trade-off between inflation and unemployment wit- nessed sharp simultaneous escalation in both! They were also being told that reflation could no longer solve unemployment problems. The time was ripe for a new economic paradigm but, in fact, what emerged was something very old and rather familiar.

The new microeconomics

The new classical theory developed mainly in the United States by Milton Friedman and others, but supported in Britain by Friedrich Hayek, may be seen as a partial reversion to the basic classical view but with the addition of a number of important refinements. In its early stages the new economics was especially noted for its emphasis on the importance of money supply – hence the term monetarism. But it also emphasized the role of the market and, over time, this has proved to be the more enduring feature.

In dealing specifically with the labour market Friedman produced in 1968 the notion of a 'natural rate' of unemployment and this is now widely accepted and used by most economists.[18] This is an equilibrium concept and the notion is that in any economy there is a rate of unemployment which is consistent with non-accelerating inflation (or deflation). It is assumed that there is a trade-off between wages (and prices) and unemployment. The 'natural rate' is defined as the non-accelerating-inflation-rate-of-unemployment or

NAIRU. This concept incorporates market imperfections and structural rigidities such as trade union power, unemployment benefits and market mismatches. Friedman and other proponents of the notion of NAIRU assume that it varies in size according to the degree of market imperfection. Thus the NAIRU is seen as an indicator of departures from perfect competition and an indicator of structural maladjustments. To use the term 'natural' in this context is highly questionable and potentially confusing. It is impossible to identify the 'natural rate' precisely and it may change at any point in time. Although the 'natural rate' hypothesis is based upon mechanistic assumptions which may be unrealistic and is at best an elusive concept, its influence on policy and economic theorizing has been considerable.

In effect it may be said that, under the influence of the new economics, the main object of economic policy has been to allow the economy to move towards the 'natural rate' while taking steps to free the market so that the 'natural rate' is reduced to as low a level as possible. Friedman argued that if governments attempted to reduce unemployment below the 'natural rate' this would lead to accelerating inflation. He made no attempt to explore the converse, but perfectly logical possibility, that attempts to push the level of unemployment above the 'natural rate' would lead to accelerating deflation. While history certainly confirms that demand expansion or contraction may have some influence in raising or lowering inflation or deflation, clear evidence of acceleration is lacking.

More recently it has been suggested that while there may be a short-term, equilibrium rate of unemployment similar to Friedman's 'natural rate', this tends to follow the actual rate of unemployment. Thus any move from the actual rate may raise or lower inflation. If the 'natural rate' of unemployment tends to follow the actual rate then clearly there may be a case for government intervention to raise aggregate demand. This essentially Keynesian concept is known as 'hysteresis' which literally means magnetism.

The new microeconomics also makes use of 'search theory' in explaining unemployment. The persistence of unemployment is explained in terms of individuals indulging in voluntary unemployment while seeking to maximize future wage income by investing in information or job search and trading wages for leisure plus unemployment benefit. Unemployment, therefore, is seen as a supply-side phenomenon.

Benjamin and Kochin used a new microeconomic approach to argue that British interwar unemployment was largely voluntary and attributable to 'generous' unemployment benefits relative to wages.[19] While this approach has been emphatically rejected[20] it undoubtedly contains a grain of truth and, in a less extreme form, the analysis might have been more constructive. Similar views in relation to unemployment in the 1980s are common. Notions that most of the mass unemployment of the interwar years and the 1980s was voluntary seem bizarre and offensive to many non-economists. Most historians would find it difficult to explain why large sections of the British workforce suddenly opted for idleness at the beginning of the 1920s and again sixty years later, while displaying a very pronounced work ethic between 1940 and 1980. In fact, use of the term 'voluntary' by economists is intended to be scientific rather than moralistic and it is assumed that the individuals concerned have made a rational economic choice in opting for leisure.

The main economic theories relating to unemployment have all been based upon a particular view of the labour market and all assume that a *general* labour market exists. The nineteenth-century classical economists assumed that there was a more or less perfect labour market with continuous wage–price adjustments. When unemployment rose above the minimal or full employment level it was eliminated by wage adjustments. Keynes perceived that from the early 1920s these adjustments no longer occurred and argued, therefore, that it was necessary to expand the economy to ensure full employment at existing wage levels. However, he did not totally reject the classical view of the labour market and certainly believed that reducing unemployment below a certain level would have inflationary consequences. More recently Friedman's ingenious 'natural rate' hypothesis reasserts the market principle and assumes a trade-off between inflation and unemployment while taking account of market imperfections and interference. Thus the new economics has been able to reassert the simple old classical ideas by insisting that they still apply in an imperfect world. Indeed, Friedman's principle of 'parsimony' completely rejects institutional and non-market influences, at least in the long run, and reasserts the fundamental market ideal in its crude form. In one of the most influential works of the 1980s Bruno and Sachs reiterate the notion that unemployment, on an international basis, is caused by wages being too high.[21] Looking at the British economy Minford suggests that in a truly free economy, with flexible wages and benefits, unemployment could be abolished. Thus he argues that society is responsible for unemployment: the unemployed, for refusing to work for lower wages; the employed for earning wages which are too high; and society, in general, for paying unemployment benefits and sanctioning other forms of market interference.[22]

During the late nineteenth century classical market theory made little sense to empirical investigators, who became well aware that involuntary unemployment could and did exist. While Keynes replaced one market analysis with another and this, in turn, was superseded by new microeconomic analysis, the dissatisfaction with market-based explanations has continued. The plain truth is that the simple notion of a labour market tends to conflict with observed reality. It is obvious that wages and employment are determined by more complex processes than simple market theories suggest and in recent years a number of new approaches have developed.[23] These reflect research and development in industrial relations and industrial sociology but economists also have sought to take account of real world departures from the classical model which assumes perfectly competitive markets in which labour is atomistic and homogeneous; also, that technology is given, rather than determined, by employers, and that firms simply act as a transmission mechanism between markets. The idea of a freely adjusting general labour market, including the employed and the unemployed, has been at least partially modified, although many economists continue to ignore this in stylized approaches which make no allowance for institutional and social processes, not to mention empirical observation.

New approaches to labour market analysis include the idea that labour markets may be 'segmented', with restrictions on entry and mobility.[24] Also that there may be an 'implicit contract' in employment relationships whereby workers trade employment stability against wage maximization. The concept of labour market 'shelters' has also been employed[25] along with the idea of 'internal' labour markets which may be occupational or firm-based.[26] The view of trade unions as monopoly sellers of labour is well established and more recently it has been suggested that unions tend to set wages while employers determine employment levels.[27] In general, it may be said that most attempts by economists to take account of real world departures from the simple classical model of the labour market have involved a reassertion of the market view in an amended form. In other words, they assert that real world phenomena, which may seem to deny the existence of a market, do no such thing. Thus Doeringer and Piore used concepts of human capital theory and internal labour markets to infer that there is a range of sub-markets which, in effect, function as a general market in the classical manner.[28] Where restrictions on competition such as racism are recognized these tend to be explained in market terms and integrated into market equilibrium theory. For example, Becker and Levy-Garbona treat race discrimination as a 'taste' in an individual utility function, so that racism can be analysed in market terms.[29] However, as Solow has suggested, 'We may predispose ourselves to misunderstanding certain aspects of unemployment if we insist on modelling the buying and selling of labour within a set of background assumptions whose main merit is that they are well adapted to models of the buying and selling of cloth.'[30] All such approaches imply empirical dissatisfaction with previous market analysis, but this is usually combined with a determination to retain it in a modified form. Increasingly, therefore, the labour market is being analysed in socio-political terms and this is providing useful new insights. At the same time, new approaches to industrial relations and management also indicate departures from simple market analysis.

The failure of wages to adjust in the 1980s has been explained through suggestions that many of the unemployed, and the long-term unemployed especially, are outside the labour market.[31] Others have suggested that society is increasingly divided into 'insiders', who can look forward to a lifetime of regular employment, and 'outsiders', who will suffer periods of unemployment and inferior employment. Not surprisingly, 'insiders' tend to be better educated and come from higher socioeconomic groups than 'outsiders'. In other words, the employment pattern reflects the power structure of society.

It appears, therefore, that the academic approach to unemployment in recent years has been in some ways ambivalent. On the one hand, the new microeconomics has established an approach which is firmly based in the belief that there is a general market for labour which works along textbook lines. On the other hand, there are new approaches which suggest a departure from this long-standing belief. At the moment these approaches are certainly not irreconcilable although they could very soon become so. In recent years the argument about unemployment has been presented as a debate between market 'reality' and unrealistic social and human aspirations which assert that unemployment is unacceptable. These opposing views have been summarized by Roger Clarke in the following way:[32]

> One school of thought, characterised by the technocrats . . . asserts that, given the present economic, demographic and global circumstances, very high levels of unemployment are inevitable. The opposing school of thought is characterised by the man on the Unemployment Rally. He is there to protest that, in the words of the United Nations Charter, 'everyone has the right to work'.

In fact, it seems that both of these points of view represent extremes which serve to cloud the real issues and prevent the emergence of solutions.

IV

The Emergence of Unemployment

'The whole form of the movement of modern industry depends, therefore, upon the constant transformation of a part of the labouring population into unemployed or half-employed hands.' *Karl Marx, 1867*

'The absurdity of labour being from time to time totally unemployed, in spite of everyone wanting more goods, can only be due to a muddle, which should be remediable if we could think and act clearly.' *J. M. Keynes, 1923*

The history of unemployment is difficult to summarize briefly because the literature on the subject is enormous and there has been a good deal of controversy. Both the output and argument seem set to continue. It may be claimed that Britain has a particular relevance to this subject because of its long industrial history and its perceived role as the cradle and social laboratory for economic theory. Britain had the first industrial revolution, which occurred spontaneously during the late eighteenth and early nineteenth centuries and, subsequently, all other nations which embarked on industrialization owed something to Britain. More recently, Britain has been seen as a pioneer of industrial maturity and of 'post-industrial society'. What is referred to as classical economic theory developed against perceptions of eighteenth- and nineteenth-century Britain. In the interwar years the evolution of Keynesian economics took place in the context of a British mass unemployment problem. From 1940 Britain led the world in its commitment to 'full employment' which was taken seriously by all shades of opinion. Under Margaret Thatcher the country has been a laboratory for monetarism and other new economic theories.

Pre-industrial society

It is often argued that unemployment is essentially a problem of industrial society and capitalism in particular, but this is clearly incorrect. At the present time in the industrialized or OECD countries there are perhaps 30 million people officially accepted as being unemployed. In the underdeveloped world, on any realistic estimate, unemployment must affect at least ten times as many people. The past has been described as 'another country' and there are many examples of worklessness in pre-industrial and ancient times.[1] The problem features in the Bible and it has been suggested that the pyramids were an early example of job creation.

Under the manorial system most people laboured to produce the food which they, their dependants and a few others would eat. The allocation of labour and product was decided according to feudal power relationships rather than market price mechanisms. In theory at least, feudalism gave everyone a job. In fact, there was never a rigid or uniform structure in Britain or even England. With the weakening of the manorial system there was a gradual drift towards wage labour. The Black Death in 1348 may have removed one-third of the workforce and this undoubtedly hastened change both in master–servant relationships and land ownership and use. By Tudor times large areas of England were being enclosed for sheep pastures and population displacement was accelerated.

In the literature of medieval and early modern Europe there is frequent reference to the existence of the poor and beggars.[2] In 1698 Vauban classified 10 per cent of the French population as beggars and 30 per cent as 'near beggars'.[3] At about the same time in England Gregory King estimated that cottagers and paupers made up 20 per cent of the population. Even in societies with widespread domestic service, large numbers were unable to obtain a livelihood.

Pre-industrial society was overwhelmingly agrarian and even in England, where textiles were important as a means of employment from the 1600s, until the nineteenth century most people worked on the land. Jan de Vries suggests that during the seventeenth century, over most of Europe, a peasant family of five, farming 20 acres might, given average yields, feed itself and one or two others.[4] In

England and the Low Countries yields were higher, but even so, most of the workforce was required simply to feed itself and its direct dependants. As a result, there was a close nexus between population and employment. If employment was prevented for some reason such as warfare, blight or adverse weather, then people starved.

Industrialization was made possible by rising agricultural productivity, especially in Britain. Industry carried productivity to new levels and the relatively close links between output, population and employment were loosened still further. Ironically, in modern industrial society unemployment is made possible by increased production and productivity and by higher incomes which enable consumption to be postponed. In a modern free market economy economic activity is the result of many individual decisions. Since most consumers are rich enough not to have to spend all their income on day-to-day or weekly requirements this generates savings which, in turn, make investment possible. Consumers and investors may delay consumption and investment. This simple fact is the basic explanation of instability in modern capitalist economies.

The creation of an industrial workforce

The British Industrial Revolution can be seen as a massive transformation in occupations or employment and it is interesting that the most recent interpretations by economic historians emphasize this aspect while playing down growth, productivity improvements and technical change which have usually received more attention.[5] The shift from rural into urban-industrial employment in Britain took place at an exceptionally early stage in economic development and, by the middle of the nineteenth century, Britain was an urban-industrial society, well ahead of any other nation with the possible exception of Belgium. The structural changes which resulted from industrialization produced dramatic changes in the employment pattern. In 1700 at least two-thirds of the workforce were directly employed in agriculture. The remainder were mainly in service industries. With the Industrial Revolution the main growth in employment was in the secondary or manufacturing sector and the proportion in agriculture declined (although absolute numbers in agriculture did not decline until after 1850). By the late nineteenth century the proportion of the workforce in manufacturing industry reached a peak at about 40 per cent. In the present century most of the growth in employment has been in the tertiary sector.

The basic explanation for these changes is in terms of income and productivity effects. As incomes increase people spend *relatively* less on food and more on manufactured goods and services. At still higher income levels services, including government, take the major part of consumer expenditure. Over time massive increases in productivity in agriculture have been possible. In 1700 perhaps 60 per cent of the workforce was needed to work directly in agriculture in order to feed the population and provide other basic requirements. By the late twentieth century Britain was producing a much greater farm output with less than 2 per cent of the workforce. Similar trends can be discerned in the secondary or manufacturing sector where productivity improvements have enabled a declining workforce (first relatively and then absolutely) to produce more. In recent years the absolute decline in the manufacturing workforce has been labelled 'de-industrialization'. This is in fact part of a process which has been developing for at least six decades and perhaps it should not cause undue alarm where it results from rapid productivity growth in manufacturing. However, in Britain since 1966 there has been an absolute decline in the manufacturing workforce of 4 million and a decline in total employment of approximately 2 million. In this period deindustrialization has been associated with stagnation in manufacturing output, a deteriorating international position and unemployment. It is, therefore, a major cause for concern.

Since the early part of this century most of the workforce has been employed in the tertiary sector and this continues to intensify. It is difficult to measure output and productivity in services and the conventional method in national income estimating is to assume that output equals nominal income, or pay (wages, salaries, profits, dividends) in the sector. It is usually assumed that productivity growth in services is relatively slow. Certainly it is difficult to conceive of acceptable ways of improving the productivity of *haute cuisine* waiters or hairdressers, but in other tertiary activities dramatic improvements have occurred. It is easy to see how the 'new technology', for example, in the form of computers or word-processors could make wide-ranging improvements which might involve major changes in the pattern of employment. The possible revolutionization of office work could mean a loss of employment for secretaries and typists who could be replaced, at least in part, by machines. So far, however, very little actual job loss has resulted from the introduction of microelectronic machines and it is important not to overemphasize the impact of micro-processing.[6] Indeed, new technology has already created many new jobs and will create many more in the future. At the present time the possible impact of 'new technology' on employment remains unclear, although there has been a good deal of speculation.[7]

The arrival of new factories and machines in the first half of the nineteenth century threatened and eventually destroyed the existing handicraft industries which were operated mainly on a domestic basis. Bythel's account of the plight of the hand-loom weavers tells how they resisted the threat, sometimes with violence, before being overwhelmed.[8] The Luddites or machine wreckers have usually been seen, in retrospect, as misguided and the term today is used in abuse. In fact they had legitimate grievances. Technical change is a feature of any modern industrial society and, in the process, particular groups may be threatened and suffer. With vested interests in particular forms of organization and technology there are forces in society which favour stagnation.[9] Technical improvements usually reduce costs of production and, as a result, income should increase. In turn this should create more demand and more employment. Certainly this has been the case in the past, although some think it may not be so in the future. Workers who become victims of technological unemployment may not be able to find an alternative form of work which is comparable. Very often there is a loss of skilled status, and relative pay, as well as employment in a traditional area. In recent years, for example, Fleet Street printers have found that, with new printing methods, far fewer people are required to produce newspapers and also that most of these are unskilled or semi-skilled. New techniques usually convey social benefit by reducing costs of production but individuals certainly suffer in the process. These problems are most easily dealt with where the demand for labour is most buoyant. Workers and unions are most likely to fear new technology when work is scarce and insecure. Employers have less economic incentive to introduce labour-saving innovations when labour is abundant. Ironically, the ability to resist innovation varies inversely with the level of employment and this may mean that employers will use recession to force change. This was so in engineering in the 1920s and in steel, coal and other industries during the 1980s. In the process there was confrontation and once-powerful unions were defeated.

What is being suggested at the present time is that 'new technology' is fundamentally different from all forms of technical change which have occurred in the past (the same was said of 'automation' in the 1950s). This dubious approach suggests that, instead of conveying general social benefits, the social costs will outweigh the benefits. These gloomy views are based on the assumption that employment opportunities will be limited to a privileged minority. History suggests that this is to underestimate both human needs and ingenuity. All previous experience suggests that major new technologies produce new lifestyles and patterns of organization. During the interwar years electricity and the motor-car produced such effects, on the one hand, replacing human and animal labour massively, and, on the other, creating great new areas of employment which were not even imagined by previous generations. History may not teach us what to predict, but it can expose the follies of prediction. Throughout British industrial history there have been dire predictions about the future effects of technical change.

With the Industrial Revolution the majority of the British population became largely if not entirely dependent upon male 'bread-winners' selling their labour for a cash wage, normally paid weekly. However, this process happened very gradually and, even at the end of the nineteenth century, there was a great deal of variation from the industrial norm. Common land rights and obligations disappeared and, as urban living became the norm, there was little opportunity to 'live off the land' and most of the necessities of life were purchased for cash. The ability to relate to the new wage system varied enormously. A small group of skilled workers enjoyed a relatively privileged position with higher wages and more regular employment. Alongside this 'labour aristocracy' was a much larger industrial workforce accustomed also to regular employment. However, the stereotype of the nineteenth-century industrial artisan should not be allowed to mislead. Larger groups of rural and urban workers earned a poorer and more haphazard existence from farm work, domestic service and less regularized activities in the tertiary sector. By the late nineteenth century this teeming mass of the 'poor' had become mainly urban and was a major cause of social concern.[10]

Industrialization imposed new life patterns and disciplines, including the 'tyranny of the clock', and an increasingly urban location for the majority.[11] The dependence upon a weekly wage income for men was overwhelming but far from total. While most single, widowed and separated women were obliged to find employment as a matter of necessity, the employment opportunities for females were severely limited by social convention and the heavy physical demands of most employment. Childbearing and rearing imposed further constraints. Female labour was heavily concentrated in a few areas; in particular, domestic service, textiles and clothing. However, women worked informally and often seasonally in agriculture and many other areas. Most women married and the established convention was that when married they only accepted paid employment where compelled to do so by outstanding necessity. This was an upper-class notion which gradually extended down the social scale. During the late nineteenth century, as living standards rose, participation rates for married women appear to have declined, although single women were more likely to be employed. However, in textile areas, where there was more availability of acceptable female employment, married women did participate rather more heavily in paid employment and had smaller families. It is possible to suggest, therefore, that British women during the nineteenth century were victims of unemployment, or limited employment opportunities, as well as social attitudes and male dominance. Dependence on men, large families and domestic drudgery reflected a limited labour market as well as social convention.[12]

They were not the only victims. Although some of the early British entrepreneurs experienced labour supply difficulties, and skilled labour was always at a premium, the nineteenth century was, in general, a period of chronic excess supply of labour.[13] Although population growth peaked in the 1830s it remained high by modern standards. Increased productivity combined with natural increase to ensure that labour demand failed to catch supply. Throughout the century unemployment, underemployment and low wages remained as the principal hazards of British working-class life and these circumstances reflected chronic excess supply of labour. This persistent tendency towards a 'reserve army' of labour was seen by Karl Marx as a product of capitalism, but subsequent history and development in other countries may suggest that this was not necessarily so.[14] However, there can be little doubt that labour surplus was an important conditioning influence on the nature and development of British industry, accounting in part for both its early success and subsequent difficulties.

In a heavily oversupplied labour market it was possible to purchase the maximum physical effort of human beings for a wage which approximated to the subsistence norm. Put more dramatically, employers who acted in purely rational economic terms had an incentive to work unskilled labour to a physiological maximum. Fortunately, the harshness of the system was constrained by both economic and non-economic factors. Subsistence had to be defined against a conventional notion of decency and there appears to have been a rising trend in material standards of living and productivity from the 1820s although we cannot be sure that the quality of life also improved.[15] Possibly there was some trade-off between income and lifestyle. Religion, paternalism and charitable tradition also provided some modification of an extremely harsh system. Workers were certainly not devoid of industrial bargaining power although this varied enormously. Nevertheless, compared both with the present and with previous periods, the nineteenth century stands out as a period of appalling physical drudgery for those lucky enough to find employment. Survival for most men depended upon being able to work incredibly long hours by modern standards. Even in the 1890s the eleven-hour day, six-day week remained common. Few societies before or since worked to such a level of physical intensity.

Within this context British working-class men did make real choices about their lives, playing their own part in creating the system. Most men opted for marriage although this often led to poverty when children arrived. Also, the majority opted for more work and a higher standard of living rather than clinging to previous patterns and standards. By the later nineteenth century materialism had fused with morality to produce a powerful work ethic. Those who endured poverty (absolute or relative) through adherence to less well paid and casual employment were often despised and compelled to harder work by social pressures as well as economic inducements. It is quite clear that the British working class was far from being passive in the evolution of capitalism.

Recognition of an unemployment problem, 1880–1914

In her study of attitudes towards unemployment in the decades before 1914 Josie Harris has indicated that there was revival of interest in the problem in the 1880s.[16] During the early 19th century economists had been concerned about the possibility of over-population and Malthus and others had debated the proposition that people would always tend to increase faster than the means of supporting life. In other words, society would always tend to have an unemployment problem.

These fears were removed by rapid economic development and overseas expansion. Public concern was also diminished because the burden on ratepayers was eased by the New Poor Law of 1834. Until the 1880s there was little public discussion and the problem of unemployment seems to have been largely ignored by economists, social reformers and politicians. Concerns which did arise, for example, during the 1840s depression or as a result of the cotton famine during the American Civil War, were seen as essentially short-run problems caused by special circumstances. The 1880s mark an important turning point in attitudes and interest in the problem. Indeed, it was only in the 1880s that the term 'unemployment' began to be used in its modern sense and applied to artisans normally in paid work but involuntarily idle. Previously it had described voluntarily idle men of means or gentlemen with no specific employment and no need of it. Thus it was possible for Victorians to describe Prince Albert as being 'unemployed' without any offence being intended or taken.

There is no strong evidence that the new interest in employment problems coincided with a change in the labour market. While the years between the 1870s and the 1890s were labelled 'the Great Depression', most economic historians now believe this was a misnomer.[17] Cyclical depressions may have become more regular after 1850 but the official unemployment statistics do not indicate an upward trend. It seems reasonable to conclude, therefore, that the new concern reflected social and political considerations rather more than economic developments. However, from the 1880s there was an increasing acceptance of the observed fact that unemployment was endemic to the system, not least because trade cycles including slumps were taking place with almost monotonous regularity. Workers unemployed during general trade depressions could not be accused of character deficiencies or voluntary idleness, especially when they resorted to protest and riot. From the 1880s the Victorian work ethic turned into demands for 'work or maintenance'. Such demands could no longer be totally ignored. The extension of the franchise to include some of those most vulnerable to loss of employment together with the growth of trade unions and new political groups which made unemployment an issue forced the employment question to the centre of the political stage. This coincided with the loss of mid-Victorian confidence and the emergence of serious misgivings in some quarters about British society, which in turn led to a questioning of *laissez-faire* capitalism. By 1914 there had been a marked change in attitudes and important new approaches had emerged at government level. Unemployment had been highlighted as a major problem and had become an important issue in public policy and administration. As a result, by the eve of the First World War, British government was committed in principle to counter cyclical public works (albeit on a voluntary, local authority basis); National Insurance gave a substantial minority some protection against unemployment; there had been efforts to stamp out casual hiring systems and Labour Exchanges had been introduced. In just thirty years there had been a pronounced shift from the *laissez-faire* philosophy of mid-Victorian Britain towards the radical idea that working-class citizens should have, perhaps, a right to 'work or maintenance'.

These changes in attitude took place without corresponding developments in economic theory. By the late nineteenth century British economics was making important new theoretical developments, but these were increasingly abstract and seemed to have little direct bearing on the real world. The earlier concern about overpopulation had given way to worries about overproduction which caused cyclical depressions, unemployment and underemployment. However, the mainstream clung to traditional classical economic views which suggested that unemployment assistance would encourage idleness and public works would poach private capital and would not lead to any increase in aggregate employment. Unemployment was seen as a problem which arose from imperfections in the labour market rather than from the nature of industrial capitalism.[18] Those who criticized the economic system, including Marx and later Hobson were treated as eccentrics and largely ignored. The term 'unemployment' was first used by Alfred Marshall, the leading classical economist, in 1888 and in the early 1890s economists began to define and classify types of unemployment.[19] The first detailed and systematic theoretical treatment by an academic economist was produced by Pigou in 1913, but this simply restated the classical concepts.[20]

Despite the absence of any significant changes in academic economics, the problem of unemployment began to be highlighted both by radicals and administrative reformers from the 1880s onwards. Britain at or near the peak of its imperial hegemony was a divided and grossly inequitable society and, for a variety of reasons, from the 1880s urban poverty became a matter of general concern and it became less easy to attribute poverty to moral failure. There was the start of a shift in emphasis in explaining poverty from character and personal factors to industrial and environmental explanations. Also, the connection between poverty and unemployment was increasingly realized. One Poor Law Inspector reported in 1887:[21]

> The large towns of England are unhappily full of a class of low, loafing, tipsy people, very different from the elite of the artisan and labouring classes, though shading gradually into them . . . the class described forms unhappily one of the largest factors in the sum total of our population . . . How to deal with it is perhaps the most important social question of the day.

This condescending attitude was not untypical. Despite the continuation of such moralistic views there was increasing realization that the undermass was created and sustained by unemployment and underemployment. The first systematic study of poverty dates from the 1880s and by the turn of the century Booth and Rowntree had demonstrated that 'want of employment' was the root cause of poverty and that poverty was very extensive. Even on the most rigorous definition, up to 40 per cent of the population lived in some degree of poverty.[22]

These essentially social and political issues began to receive increasing attention. Radicals ranging across the political spectrum inevitably addressed themselves to the problem and argued their particular solutions. Socialists saw unemployment as an essential feature of capitalism and protectionists, single-taxers and underconsumptionists also blamed the system. Empire settlement was widely and increasingly advocated also. None of these solutions found favour with authority. The overwhelming balance of political and economic opinion remained against economic intervention.

During the 1880s there was agitation by the unemployed which was both organized and spontaneous. Mass demonstrations by and on behalf of the unemployed became a regular feature from this time, especially in London, and were organized by trade unions and such groups as the Social Democratic Federation.[23] There were major demonstrations in 1892–3 and in 1903. These included frequent allegations of police brutality as well as 'invasions' of the most select areas of the West End of London and occasions of riot. Local authorities, especially in metropolitan areas, became increasingly concerned with the problem and there was a Poor Law crisis from the 1880s associated with rising costs and harsher administration. Most of the able-bodied unemployed did not use the Poor Law except in the most extreme desperation, but some outdoor relief had continued after 1834. From the 1880s the authorities attempted to eliminate all traces of this and became stricter even though public pressure to make provision for unemployment was growing.

Between 1886 and 1893 the so-called 'Chamberlain Circular' was issued by central government to local authorities five times. This urged public works during periods of depression but provided no central government funds. There was no particular novelty about this and it does not appear to have had much effect. Widespread relief works were undertaken by local authorities, for example, in 1892–3, but this was a long-established practice. Indeed it has been suggested that the circulars enabled Poor Law authorities to move responsibility to local councils.[24] In the 1890s attempts to establish a 'right to work' through local authority relief works, especially in London boroughs such as West Ham, failed. Local authorities in poor areas lacked the resources to fulful such a role. Indeed, the ability was least likely to occur where it was most needed because of the local taxation system, and there was no question of central government support. Inevitably, the initiative and attention moved increasingly towards central government.

In 1895–6 a *Select Committee on Distress from Want of Employment* had been appointed in the hope that a way could be found to reform the administration of unemployment relief. Although the Committee gathered useful evidence on the causes of unemployment it

[63]

had little impact. The Poor Law system remained as an inadequate ultimate resort. Local authority works had some success but fell far short of a solution and were increasingly frowned upon by sections of Whitehall as radical local authorities emerged. Heavy reliance on charity and 'self-help' continued. In 1905 the Unemployed Workmen Act attempted, in more formal terms, what had been intended in the Chamberlain Circulars. The intention was also to bolster and rationalize relief and the efforts of Poor Law and other local authorities. Small central government grants were provided for from 1906. In general the Act served to discredit further any line of approach through local authorities and charities and the arguments for a national system gained support.[25]

With the Liberal landslide of 1906 the way was paved for a new approach to unemployment through administrative reforms. Politically this was spearheaded by Winston Churchill and David Lloyd George who saw reform as essential if more radical political developments were to be prevented. Unemployment became a national issue for public policy and administration rather than being left entirely to local authorities. The Liberals aimed at a 'scientific solution' which, initially, was intended to improve the labour market while at the same time developing the apparatus for central government control. The approach relied heavily on ideas and information supplied by pragmatic reformers such as Beveridge, Booth, Llewellyn Smith and the Webbs and the actual reforms related primarily to the formal employment of skilled and semi-skilled men in the major industries. They addressed, in particular, the problem of cyclical unemployment as it affected the upper echelons of the manual workforce. In general the main thrust of the Liberal reforms had the effect of removing certain 'deserving' groups from the danger of having to rely on the Poor Law. However, the Poor Law remained and there was no attempt to tackle the main sources of poverty. Endemic unemployment and underemployment in the undermass were not really addressed by the main Liberal reforms and areas such as casual, juvenile and female labour were not much affected although they gained some attention. Three major administrative reforms resulted. These were

Labour Exchanges, the National Insurance Scheme (NIS) and the Development Act which provided central government funds for counter-cyclical public works.

Although Beveridge has been credited with the idea of Labour Exchanges they had been suggested before and were in use elsewhere.[26] The Labour Exchange Bill was introduced in 1909 and there were 423 exchanges in use by 1914, but the system fell far short of organizing the labour market along the lines which Beveridge intended. Similarly, the employment provisions of the National Insurance Act of 1911 were intended to penalize irregular work and hiring, but failed to do so because of widespread resistance and evasion. Nevertheless the limited NIS Scheme (see Chapter V for details) was judged to be a success, not least in financial terms, and there was little resistance to future extensions in 1916 and 1920. Again, the idea of national insurance was not especially novel and there were well-established schemes in other countries. However, in Britain there was widespread insurance provision by trade unions and the private sector and the notion of a state provision was seen by some as an unwelcome extension of government and an additional form of taxation. Beveridge seems to have been aware of the administrative potential and the connection with exchanges which was developed later.[27] In fact, the limited scheme which commenced in 1913 eventually expanded to become the main institutional feature of the British welfare system.

The Development Act of 1909 attempted to apply the views of the Minority Report of the Royal Commission on the Poor Law which had been written by the Webbs and urged that public funds should be used to regulate the level of economic activity through the provision of counter-cyclical public works.[28] In fact, there was a long tradition of public works in Britain and, despite the absence of support from theoretical economics, the provision had been increasing since 1870. In the Edwardian period support for public works appears to have grown across the political spectrum and Lloyd George put forward a programme for a development fund to finance roads, experimental farming, forestry, coastal protection and scientific research. The Development Act of 1909 appeared to embrace a number of ideas which had gained momentum during the previous decade and it also represented a move in the direction of the establishment of a 'right to work'. However, the Act failed to provide adequate machinery for implementation and the Development Commission spent only 5 per cent of its allocation of £12 million between 1910 and 1915. Administrative problems and fears about increased public spending defeated its objects.

The Liberal reforms were essentially cautious and pragmatic but, as Harris has suggested:

> Both Churchill and Lloyd George originally saw these three measures – the Labour Exchanges Act, the National Insurance Act and the Development Act – as part of a much wider programme of social reform, which would ultimately revolutionise the relationship between the worker and the state. Lloyd George at least in private admitted that he saw insurance merely as a transitional measure, and hinted at the recognition of some kind of 'Right to Work'.[29]

In fact, the Liberal measures, very soon after their enactment, met circumstances which had not been envisaged. First, full-scale war and full employment, followed by the prolonged mass unemployment of the interwar period.

V

Interwar Unemployment: A New Dimension

'. . . the late twenties and thirties were characterized by high and rising real income, and the high unemployment at those times was the consequence almost solely of the dole. The army of the unemployed standing watch in Britain at the publication of the *General Theory* was largely a volunteer army.'   *Daniel K. Benjamin and Levis A. Kochin, 1979*

'They had been brought up to work, and behold! it seemed as if they were never going to have the chance of working again. In these circumstances it was inevitable, at first, that they should be haunted by a feeling of personal degradation. That was the attitude towards unemployment in those days: it was a disaster which happened to *you* as an individual and for which *you* were to blame.'   *George Orwell, 1936*

Although mass unemployment is usually associated most particularly with the 1930s it was a feature of the British economy for the two decades from 1920. The events of the interwar years unfolded against a grim background of high and continuous unemployment which, on the official annual figures, always affected at least 10 per cent of the workforce, averaged 14 per cent, and rose as high as 23 per cent in 1931. It has been suggested that these official statistics are potentially misleading and they should not be used to make direct comparisons with official figures for other periods.[1]

During the First World War full employment developed as demand for labour outstripped supply and this continued after 1918 in a postwar boom based on wartime savings and replacement demand. The boom broke in a sudden, severe, downturn beginning in 1920 and coinciding with a government policy initiative designed to combat inflation by cutting public spending and raising interest rates with the ultimate objective of restoring Britain to the international gold standard. There was a massive rise in unemployment to levels near 20 per cent, on the official figures, during some months of 1920. Although there was a downward movement from this peak, unemployment remained stubbornly high by previous standards and was especially heavy in areas and among workers who had' not previously experienced persistent employment problems. With the onset of world depression in 1929 there was another strong upward movement in unemployment which peaked in 1931–2. Britain suffered less from world depression than most countries and recovery in the 1930s was strong and well sustained. However, the official figure for unemployment remained over the 10 per cent level throughout. In the late 1930s the world economy appeared to falter once again and most people in Britain had come to accept heavy unemployment as a fact of life. In 1940, with the war effort in top gear, the problem disappeared and mass unemployment was not seen again in Britain until the 1970s.

The interwar experience with unemployment must be viewed as one of the most important formative experiences in modern British history. This was not because of the economic impact of unemployment. On most of the usual indicators the British economy performed reasonably well with both industry and the economy as a whole moving to higher growth rates than in the Edwardian period.[2] Nevertheless, the popular perception at least after 1940, was that these were 'wasted years' and that the system as a whole had failed. In fact, the view that the economy did well was only presented in the 1960s by historians who gave particular attention to new quantitative estimates. These were not necessarily wrong, but the point is that concern about unemployment went much deeper than a desire for regular growth in GNP. There was concern for the social and political effects of unemployment and, in particular, about its impact on some of the oldest industrial communities in the country. The failure was perceived not as a failure to produce but as an inability to sustain the social and political structure. Internally unemployment seemed to question and potentially to threaten the socioeconomic system which had made Britain the most powerful nation on earth for a time. Externally Britain's new industrial–

economic weaknesses and frustrations appeared to be underlined by the unemployment problem. These weaknesses made Britain more interested in developing its imperial connections but unemployment severely limited the possibilities. The white dominions were no longer willing to accept large numbers of British emigrants, even though British governments were willing to subsidize such traffic for the first time. The dominions, with their own concerns about employment, were also unwilling to allow free access to British goods. In 1932 at Ottawa it proved possible to exchange mutual preferences, but these were established by raising duties against non-empire producers rather than through the reduction of trade barriers within the empire. Empire free trade was no longer a possibility.

Victorian and Edwardian portents

We know now that during the late nineteenth century Britain commenced a process of relative economic decline which has tended to continue ever since. Over the last hundred years Britain's standard of living, measured conventionally in terms of GNP per head, has grown less than that of other industrial nations – probably without exception. During the past two decades this phenomenon of relative economic decline has been given increasing attention and it may be said that reversing the decline is now very definitely on the political agenda. The precise reasons for decline remain obscure, despite much academic attention.[3] There are some grounds for questioning the extent of suggested decline and the statistics which purport to measure it. Some have suggested that relative decline may have been inevitable and unavoidable and it seems probable that British growth rates were always low by modern standards and in terms of international comparison.[4] The view persists that Britain could have done better. In theory any industrial nation which had ample supplies of labour and capital should have been able to stay ahead of the field by adopting appropriate technologies and policies. This implies that Britain squandered the advantages of an early start and lost its pre-eminent position by neglect. More recently the problem has been seen in terms of a failure to reduce the massive lag which has now opened up between Britain and the most advanced industrial nations in terms of technology, productivity and incomes.

Britain's problems can be traced back to the late nineteenth century but they were not much noticed at the time. Although new industries failed to develop as widely and as rapidly as elsewhere, the traditional manufacturing industries continued to be prosperous even though they were sometimes slow in developing the latest technologies.[5] In the Edwardian period there was a sharp deceleration in rates of growth of real income per head and in industrial productivity.[6] This slowdown had international dimensions but only Britain came near stagnation. It has been suggested that the failure to develop new industries may be partially explained through the notion of a 'low-wage-low-productivity trap'.[7] The suggestion is that a vicious circle of low wages, limited markets and domestic investment opportunities inhibited industrial initiative and structural change. By the end of the nineteenth century British industry was using labour, and skilled labour especially, in a relatively intensive way and it was increasingly dependent on cheap industrial labour. In turn this dictated a low wage situation. In particular, this was the case in what have been called the 'old staple' industries which had pioneered the Industrial Revolution and included coal, cotton, iron and steel, shipbuilding and heavy engineering.

The new growth industries of the early twentieth century such as motor vehicles required a prosperous home market in order to become established on a mass production basis. British income levels and distribution effects provided only limited scope for such industries. While Britain developed simple consumer goods such as toilet soap and biscuits, the United States, with higher per capita income levels, was developing mass production motor vehicles. Skilled labour in Britain remained relatively abundant and cheap and much of British industry continued to use it intensively and labour-saving technology was sometimes ignored. This may have maximized profits in the short run but in the long run British industry found it harder to compete.

The pattern of industrial organization and management which

had emerged in Britain by 1914 had been conditioned most heavily by cheap and ample labour supply and export orientation. Both of these influences made sophisticated company structures and techniques of management unnecessary. Since such a high proportion of product was exported it was assumed that markets could not be controlled, although differentiation of products was possible. Home markets also remained relatively competitive by international standards and production units remained typically small despite the late nineteenth-century merger movement. Labour management was also neglected although there was a great deal of paternalism. Cheap labour and the plentiful supply of skill created a tradition whereby British employers ignored and neglected education and training both directly, through their own efforts, and indirectly, through the state and other agencies. Only a few, highly exceptional employers developed labour market strategies to improve the quality of labour supply and to retain labour over long periods. The small family firm remained typical although a few loose conglomerates had been created by 1900. Typically, employers expectd to be able to hire and fire labour as they required and internal labour markets were highly unusual. Training was left in large part to the craft unions who controlled entry through seven-year apprenticeships. British governments were not pressured in any sustained way by the business community to improve technical education, or education in general.[8] Indeed the business lobby was ever conscious of the need to minimize local government rates and taxation in general. Also, they failed to influence other educational institutions including private schools and universities. As a result of the comparative neglect of secondary, technical and tertiary education Britain gradually forfeited its technological lead and the superiority of its human capital, so evident in the years before 1870, was not sustained.

Britain's loss of industrial leadership has recently been attributed to non-economic factors by Martin Weiner who stresses cultural influences which amount, in essence, to a contempt for industry and commerce and the pursuit of profit.[9] For centuries the dominant success image in Britain has been and remains, it is claimed, the unworldly, rural gentleman making a virtue of voluntary idleness. However, similar heroes can be found in all European societies and the thesis, despite its eloquent pleading, fails to explain why Britain became the workshop of the world in the first place. In fact the influence of material necessity and economic motivation is clearly evident and continues to be evident in British history. McCloskey and others have attempted to show that British entrepreneurs, in the main, acted rationally and, therefore, that Victorian Britain did not 'fail'.[10] Not only were businessmen perfectly rational in deciding whether or not to adopt new technology, the economy did just about as well as it possibly could have given available supplies of labour and capital. In particular, this view rests upon an assumption that resources, including labour, were fully employed and that there was little scope for diversion to more productive areas. In the light of what has been said about the late nineteenth-century labour market this assumption has to be questioned.

In whatever way we decide to assess their disappointing performance, it is clear that the Victorian and Edwardian economies continued to depend very heavily on the old staples for output, employment and export earnings. In turn, these industries became increasingly dependent on vulnerable overseas markets and relatively cheap industrial labour. The First World War accelerated changes which were probably inevitable, but all the more dramatic because they came quickly. At the end of the postwar boom in 1920 the extent of these changes, which had been masked by war, began to become clear. From this time the old staples were in crisis and they were the primary source of interwar unemployment.

Explaining the interwar unemployment problem

There have been many attempts to explain Britain's unemployment problem in the interwar period. Different explanations usually reflect different theoretical approaches. Economic debate between Keynes and classical economists raged at the time and there is similar controversy today which is reflected in approaches to history. The interwar debate was resolved in the 1940s with what seemed, on the surface at least, to be a total victory for Keynesianism. Until the

1970s most historians saw the interwar unemployment problem in simple black and white terms with Keynes as the hero and the Treasury as the villain. It was widely believed that because of economic dogma in the Treasury and elsewhere Britain had suffered two decades of misery which could have been avoided if only Keynesian policies had been accepted. Adherence to the outmoded classical view had prevented British governments from reflating the economy and eradicating unemployment. This quintessentially Keynesian view ascribed enormous influence to economic ideas and policy.[11]

In the 1970s this approach began to be questioned on both empirical and theoretical grounds.[12] The new classical economics rapidly provided new avenues of approach and the econometric techniques, which had become commonplace in economics, began to be applied to historical data. By the late 1980s the old Keynesian orthodoxy had been shattered, although it still claimed many adherents, and both historians and economists had developed a multiplicity of explanations for unemployment. Some still argued that 'demand deficiency' was the main cause[13] but new supply-side approaches suggested that unemployment was caused by unemployment benefits being too generous[14] and by wages being too high.[15] Some approaches combined both demand and supply-side influences[16] and Glynn and Booth suggested that monocausal or single explanation approaches to the problem were unlikely to be correct since the evidence suggested that there were multiple causes. This debate seems set to continue, fuelled by new developments in economic theory and historical research.

While making a number of important qualifications, Glynn and Oxborrow suggest the following explanatory approach to interwar unemployment:

> As a simplification, it is possible to think in terms of a hard core of structural unemployment, involving on average approximately 6 per cent of the insured workforce, which persisted throughout most of the interwar period. If we add to this the fairly persistent levels of seasonal and frictional

unemployment, which may have amounted to 3 or 4 per cent of the insured workforce, this would explain the interwar minimum levels of about 10 per cent. Superimposed upon these types of unemployment were varying levels of cyclical unemployment which was most intense in 1921 and during the depression period 1929–33.[17]

These views have been echoed by Stephen Constantine and others.

In fact, it is impossible to distinguish different types of unemployment with any degree of precision. Nevertheless, the above approach does serve to emphasize the fact that there was a persistent, hard core of structural unemployment throughout the interwar years. This was centred in the 'old staple' industries which may have contributed directly up to half of total unemployment during the best years of the period.[18] These industries had been central to the Industrial Revolution and they continued to dominate the economy in terms of employment and exports. They were concentrated on or near the major coalfields of Britain in south Wales, Lancashire, west Yorkshire, Tyneside and central Scotland. Ireland's main industrial centre in Belfast, although less substantial, should also be included in this list. The most important staple industries were coal, cotton and other textiles, heavy engineering, shipbuilding and iron and steel, but several others could be included. These industries had supplied the overwhelming portion of British visible exports and they continued to do so during the interwar years. As a result of the First World War they experienced a phase of rapid expansion which continued during the postwar boom. Unfortunately, this expansion left them ill-equipped to meet adverse developments which had been accelerated by war. The basic problem, and this became evident most clearly from 1920, was loss of overseas markets as a result of competition, especially from the United States and Japan, and import replacement in traditional overseas markets.

To illustrate these developments we will take the case of Australia, which, before 1914, had been a prosperous and largely open market for British exports. As a result of war the Australian market became chronically undersupplied as British industrial efforts and supply lines were diverted and the acute shipping shortage made supply impossible even where goods could be obtained. As a result Australia had to rely either on Britain's trade rivals, notably the United States and Japan, or upon its own devices. American and Japanese output and exports expanded dramatically. In Australia new industrial initiatives were launched during the war including the beginnings of steel manufacture by the BHP Company.[19] By the early 1920s Australia had embarked upon a new policy of industrial protection to preserve and enhance its fledgling industries which were increasingly seen as essential to the provision of employment for Australians. New Australian tariffs were introduced to enable Australian industries to compete against British goods although Britain continued to urge free trade. This policy made it both essential and attractive for British firms to invest directly in Australia by establishing subsidiaries to supply the Australian market. In the interwar years many important British firms ceased to supply the Australian market from Britain, opening subsidiaries in Australia which enjoyed high profit margins behind tariff barriers designed to protect inefficient domestic producers. There were similar developments in other traditional market areas, including India, and, as a result, British workers suffered rather more than British employers.

Markets were lost because of disruption and rising trade barriers resulting from tariffs and other devices. These new trade restrictions, which were often prompted by war, continued during the depressed years of the 1930s. However, the problems of British industry did not result simply from trade barriers. Technical and economic changes meant that many were less able to compete in world markets. While obsolescence and substitution affected some industries others were simply inefficiently run. There were already some signs of technological backwardness in British industry before the war and signs of an increasing dependence upon markets in less developed areas, including the empire. British management techniques lagged behind those elsewhere, notably the United States, and industrial leaders tended to be complacent and conservative. The continued domination by family firms inhibited the growth of professional management and the abundance of labour made labour market strategies seem unnecessary. During the war and postwar boom British prices and wages rose dramatically, and rather faster than elsewhere. The main reason for this was poor economic management during the war period – producing heavy indebtedness and inflation that priced British goods out of some overseas markets. Although real wages failed to be maintained during the war, they rose strongly in the postwar boom and the sharp reduction in the conventional working week during 1919–20 also added significantly to manufacturers' unit costs.[20]

By the 1920s, therefore, the most important part of the British economy, in terms of output, employment and exports, faced some serious problems. These problems did not emanate from any single cause although the results could be summed up in terms of loss of markets, and especially overseas markets. However, there was no single or simple solution. Wage cuts might have priced some goods back into some overseas markets, but not where there was deliberate trade restriction and where tariffs could be varied according to the strength of competition. In some industries, such as textiles, cheaper labour could not hope to compete with even cheaper labour elsewhere. In retrospect it is easy to say that old industries had to be replaced by new. In the future the solution to the problems of the 1980s will be equally obvious, but at the time there was no real alternative to the existing industries which continued to dominate the economy.[21] Internationally, Britain's comparative advantage remained heavily based in the staple industries. While many new industries did develop and existing ones expanded, this was insufficient to solve the unemployment problem. In fact, none of the staple industries, apart from shipbuilding, experienced a dramatic decline in output. The brunt of economic adversity was carried by the labour force in terms of unemployment. Industries in the face of adversity made themselves more efficient, often by shedding labour, and attempted to maintain profits by cutting margins and seeking state assistance. They also relied more on a prosperous and protected home market as well as developing profitable overseas subsidiaries in many cases.

The decline of the staple industries was the most enduring influence on interwar unemployment but there were others including the sharp cyclical downturns of 1921 and 1929–33. Also, labour supply into formal employment appears to have been exceptionally high as a result of relatively high birth rates during the Edwardian period. Similar demographic influences may have affected the labour market in the 1980s. Birth rates in the interwar years were sharply lower than before and it is clear that the ratio of workers, or potential workers, to dependants became unusually high with relatively few child and elderly dependants.[22] Also, women married later during the interwar years and young, single women were conventionally regarded as part of the labour market. Potentially, therefore, interwar Britain had a highly productive population but this enhanced capacity was, to some extent, wasted through unemployment.

Improvements in technology and labour productivity may also have contributed to the unemployment problem. Most improvements were undramatic and gradual but virtually all industries, including those in decline, shared in this progress. The gradual introduction of electricity to industry was one of the more obvious changes, but a host of less well known technical improvements contributed more. There were also changes in organization and not all improvement required new investment. In many of the older industries there were sharp reductions in capacity as firms and plants closed down. In theory the least efficient should have been eliminated but, in fact, this was not the case. In cotton, for example, it was the most highly indebted, including some very progressive firms, which tended to fail. This story was repeated in the 1980s. In some industries, notably engineering, unemployment enabled employers to reassert the 'right to manage' in the face of weakened trade unions. Of course, the actual process of shedding labour improved productivity since employers naturally attempted to remove the least efficient. Most cricket captains could improve batting averages by playing only their best seven men and leaving the rest in the pavilion. It is difficult to make any judgement about how much productivity changes contributed to unemployment. On balance, productivity improvements were probably the result rather than the cause of unemployment.

Inevitably any discussion of interwar unemployment must give a good deal of attention to government policy. In general, British governments in this period have been condemned more for what they failed to do than for what they actually did. Any view of government policy must be derived from economic diagnosis which involves a theory about the causes of unemployment. If we look at what government actually did it is possible to list actions which may have increased or decreased the level of unemployment. On the negative side many, and certainly most Keynesians, would include cuts in spending, balanced budgets, adherence to the gold standard in the 1920s and the imposition of high interest rates in order to do so. On the positive side it could be said that governments maintained business confidence, with one important lapse in the financial crisis of 1931, through tight budgetary policy; there were public works which employed large numbers although these did not give a net boost to the economy; in the 1920s transference policies aimed to take workers to jobs in other areas, while in the 1930s cheap money, tariffs, exchange depreciation and rearmament may have had beneficial effects on employment. Government action was not the principal cause of interwar unemployment but in the 1920s at least it seems likely that it was an aggravating factor. In the 1930s Britain fared better than most countries and government action may have played some small part in this.[23]

The policy dimension of interwar economic management is largely apolitical in the sense that both Labour and Conservative governments followed fundamentally similar policies and both stand condemned for the failure to develop alternatives. There were two minority Labour Governments in 1924 and 1929–31, both led by Ramsay MacDonald. The aim of the first was to establish that Labour could form an alternative administration without threatening the economic and political structure. In 1929 the second Labour Government reaped the whirlwind of world depression and eventually disintegrated in disagreements about cutting public spending, including unemployment benefits. Labour tried to increase public works, but the Labour Chancellor, Phillip Snowden, insisted upon a 'sound money' approach, including strict attempts to balance the budget. In 1930 a junior minister in the second Labour Government, Sir Oswald Mosley, presented the Cabinet with an ambitious blueprint for dealing with unemployment. The 'Mosley Memorandum' was rejected although it had much to commend it. The TUC consistently pressed for public works and the development of trade with Russia but also failed to develop a coherent and effective policy response to unemployment. Indeed, the trade unions were accused of neglecting the unemployed throughout the period. Wal Hannington's National Unemployed Workers' Movement (NUWM), along with other left-wing groups, was shunned and excluded.

As indicated above, until recently most approaches to the interwar unemployment problem adopted a Keynesian view and inevitably condemned government for failing to take steps to raise the level of aggregate demand in the economy. Thus, interwar governments have been accused of gross neglect and this has normally been attributed to the power of classical economic views which dominated the Treasury and the Bank of England. In the early 1970s mild criticism of this approach on empirical rather than theoretical grounds produced strong reaction.[24] However, from the late 1970s changes in economic theory began to have some impact.[25] In its earlier versions the new economics placed much emphasis on monetary factors. It is generally agreed that these had only limited effects in interwar Britain. The restrictiveness and high interest rates of the 1920s gave way to the 'cheap money' of the 1930s, but unemployment remained stubbornly high. As the attention turned from monetarism to market economics new interpretations began to appear, often supported by econometric manipulations of data which, in themselves, were controversial. Since the new economics favoured private sector solutions and saw little scope for state action it is not surprising that the main influence was in producing versions of history which justified the *status quo* rather than favouring an alternative policy regime. In other words, it was suggested that high unemployment resulted from circumstances rather than government neglect. Thus, Benjamin and Kochin argue that unemployment was essentially voluntary and resulted from generous unemployment benefits (although if this was the case it must have resulted from state action).[26] Beenstock and others attribute increased unemployment to rises in labour supply induced by higher wages. This emphasis on wages has been taken up by many commentators and there is no doubt that the focus on wages reflects the new concern with market economics.

Unemployment relief

Victorian Britain made virtually no collective provisions for social welfare apart from the New Poor Law of 1834. This was designed to cater for the relatively small number of people who became both destitute and desperate, while at the same time making no threats to the free market system. Under the New Poor Law, Poor Law rates were levied in each district and the system was locally financed and run by locally appointed guardians. Those who obtained 'poor relief' were only supposed to do so under the principle of 'less eligibility' which held that what the Poor Law provided must always be worse than could be obtained elsewhere. In other words, poor relief must not threaten wages and the able-bodied poor must be forced to price themselves into employment. Accepting poor relief carried a great social stigma and the notion that respectable working-class people did not resort to the workhouse was firmly established to such an extent that most families would endure extreme hardship and explore every alternative avenue before seeking assistance from the parish.[27]

In theory, relief was only given in the workhouse (the 'workhouse test') where conditions were degrading. By the late nineteenth century it was clearly established that the Poor Law was only for society's most unfortunate: largely, in fact, the indigent, who were too old, young, sick or feeble-minded to fend for themselves and who had no family or friends to support them. In practice, during periods of regular trade depression, many working men and their families had, in fact, been forced to resort to the Poor Law and outdoor relief had been given on these occasions. This was frowned upon by the authorities and during the late nineteenth century there was a determined campaign to eliminate outdoor relief. This coincided with increased concern about unemployment and dissatisfaction with the Poor Law system. The notion that respectable working men might become used to regular resort to public assistance as a result of cyclical economic influences worried the Government which saw the system as an important means of social regulation. In his circular to Boards of Guardians, first issued in 1886, Joseph Chamberlain urged the provision of public works during trade depressions on the grounds that: 'It is not desirable that the working classes should be familiarised with Poor Law relief, and if once the honourable sentiment which now leads them to avoid it is broken down it is probable that recourse will be had to this provision on the slightest occasion.'[28]

These attitudes continued after 1914, but from the late nineteenth century the belief that more must be done for the less fortunate tended to grow inexorably and 'respectable' working men began to demand 'work or maintenance'. By 1950 Britain had established a welfare state which aimed to provide decent minimum standards for all 'from the cradle to the grave'. The interwar period marks a transition phase in the evolution of social policy between the harsh and rudimentary Victorian Poor Law and the modern welfare state.

There was a strong tradition of charity in Victorian society and by 1900 this was being channelled into a desire to develop and pursue more formal solutions to deprivation. At the same time, the introduction of significant items of social provision did not come until after the extension of the franchise to working-class voters and after the arrival of the Labour Party on the political scene. The first major steps came with the Liberal reforms of 1906–12 which included the formal establishment of limited provisions for old age pensions and national insurance as well as a determined first move towards a more progressive taxation system.

Victorian values had been based on the belief that the free market system maximized income and wealth and that the role of government should be confined to a few minimal instances of regulation and to the traditional functions of defence and protecting private property. The role of the Poor Law was to prevent extreme cases of destitution while providing incentives to individual effort and 'self-help'. By the early twentieth century serious doubts were beginning to emerge about the viability of the system. As a means of achieving social stability and 'national efficiency' it appeared progressively less effective, while the 'fairness' of the distribution of income and wealth was increasingly open to question. In the twentieth century the extension of social welfare is essentially a question of changing perceptions of possibilities. In the Edwardian period Lloyd George and others perceived that very modest increases in welfare could be granted at the expense of the wealthiest sections of society. The implicit attitude was that redistribution to promote social welfare could not be pushed to the point where it threatened the social and economic fabric and produced political collapse. In part the alternative was to attempt to redistribute income *within* the poorer sections of society – from the healthy to the sick, from the young to the old, and from those in employment to the unemployed. This involved using the insurance principle as well as progressive taxation. Both were unpopular. In fact, the Liberal reforms were only achieved through political confrontation and crisis which resulted from proposals to increase taxation of the rich. On the eve of the First World War it was widely believed that reform had been radical and had gone to the margins of possibility; to push things further might result in breakdown. Within a year or so, war had transformed expectations once again by raising both levels of taxation and notions of the scope for state action. Lloyd George's wartime promises of a 'land fit for heroes' both built upon and lifted expectations. With the radical extension of the franchise in 1918 and extensive wartime planning for a state-orchestrated postwar reconstruction, sweeping changes seemed inevitable after the war. It is usually assumed that these failed to materialize for political and economic reasons: the election of a largely Conservative coalition in 1918 swamped most of the political enthusiasm while the problem of war debts, added to more general economic concerns after 1919, dictated government caution. The 'Geddes Axe', which was a round of government spending cuts imposed in 1921–2, is usually seen as the end to any hopes of major welfare reform after the war.[29]

In fact, there was a sharp increase in government involvement and spending on social services during the interwar period. Compared with pre-1914, government spending roughly doubled. There was more redistribution through taxation than in 1914 and social insurance was massively extended. Throughout the interwar years the major item of attention in social policy was relief for the unemployed; that is, the provision for those who were described during the nineteenth century as the 'able-bodied poor'. There were two aspects to this question: first, what right had the unemployed and their dependants to support from the rest of society? Secondly, if support was to be given, what form should it take and at what level should it be set?

In the early 1920s it appears to have become clearly established that most unemployed workers were entitled to support provided that their lack of work, and therefore income, arose from circumstances beyond their control; in other words, unemployment had to be involuntary and those receiving support had to be willing to take any reasonable offer of work. It was also established by the early 1920s that, at least for the majority of unemployed, the Poor Law was inadequate and inappropriate and an alternative had to be found. This represented a major change from the nineteenth-century situation and the essential steps will be examined below. Departure from the Poor Law necessitated new methods of funding relief and raised the possibilities that benefits could exceed wages and might be given to those who did not really need them. These were controversial matters and the question of the nature and level of support remained a matter for almost continuous debate throughout the interwar years. Unemployment relief was also a matter of political contention between the parties, the subject of several high-level public enquiries and, on occasion, the principal issue in public protest, agitation and riot.[30]

With the onset of mass unemployment in the early 1920s, the progression towards state support for the unemployed, which had commenced only a decade earlier, was rapidly completed. Interwar unemployment could not be labelled voluntary or undeserving since it affected the traditional industrial centres and the most respectable sections of the British working class. Also, it was clear that not to provide for the unemployed might have serious political consequences.

The National Insurance Act of 1911 established contributary and compulsory health insurance for most wage-earners. Part 2 of the Act provided for an experimental and limited scheme for insurance against unemployment. This applied to only 2.25 million workers, nearly all men, in certain 'scheduled trades' noted for fluctuations in employment. The scheme affected mechanical engineering, shipbuilding, iron foundries, vehicle building, construction and sawmilling. Workers, employers and the state all made contributions and the adult benefit was about 20 per cent of average male weekly earnings in 1913 when the first benefits were paid by Labour Exchanges and trade unions. No allowances were paid for dependants and benefits were intended simply as a supplement to savings rather than as a substitute for wages. Even so, there were strict limitations on entitlement to benefits. One week's benefit could be paid for five weekly contributions, but there was to be a maximum payment of fifteen weeks' benefit in any one year. Applicants had to establish entitlement and had to be capable of work but unable to obtain suitable employment.

This limited and cautious scheme was the pilot for the NIS which has continued in Britain since 1911. All sections of society including taxpayers, employers, trade unions and the workers affected had reservations about the new scheme and the compulsory element was unpopular. Nevertheless, the scheme proved acceptable and was soon judged to be a success by the authorities. In 1914 the Act was amended and a six-day waiting period for benefits was introduced; also, provision was made for linking periods of unemployment so that some forms of 'short time' could be covered. In 1916 the scheme was extended to munitions and other industries despite keen resistance and membership rose to nearly 4 million, including over 1 million women.

There was a major change in 1920–1 when national insurance was extended to a majority of the workforce and covered 12 million workers out of a workforce of 19 million. During the interwar period there existed, in effect, three avenues of relief for the unemployed:

(1) *The National Insurance Scheme* – for those covered by the 1911 Act and later extensions. Under this scheme benefits were paid as of right for limited periods for those qualified by virtue of previous contributions.

(2) *The Dole* (under various titles: Out-of-Work Donation, Uncovenanted Benefit, Extended Benefits, Transitional Benefits, National Assistance, Supplementary Benefits, Income Support) – for those who had exhausted NIS benefits or had failed to qualify for them. Provisions and regulations changed many times but from the beginning in 1918 this was seen as an alternative to the Poor Law.

(3) *The Poor Law* – until 1937 this remained as the last resort for those who failed to qualify for (1) and (2) or exhausted their entitlements.

We are dealing with a changing and complex system with areas of overlap between different forms of relief. Unemployed workers passed from one area to another and, in some cases, benefited under more than one heading.

The 'dole' originated from the 'out-of-work donation' which was intended to provide subsistence for ex-servicemen over limited periods of unemployment on leaving the armed forces. This emergency provision was promised in 1915 and operated from 1918 to 1921. When the dole was originally promised the authorities were mindful of the turbulent period which followed the end of the Napoleonic Wars in 1815. By 1918 there were additional reasons for concern about the impending demobilization of over 4 million men. The ending of munitions production also threatened to be disruptive and it seemed both unreasonable and impractical to deny the dole to many categories of civilians. By the early part of 1919, therefore, unemployment benefits on a needs basis, including dependants' allowances, were being paid without regard to insurance entitlements. In other words, unemployment benefits were being paid as of right on a needs basis to many of the unemployed and a very important concession had been made and a major precedent set. Benefits commenced at 24s (£1.20) weekly for men with 6s (30p) for the first child and 3s (15p) for subsequent children. At this time benefits under the NIS were only 7s (35p) weekly with no dependants' allowances. The scheme was administered through Labour Exchanges (renamed Employment Exchanges in 1916) and, from the beginning, it was seen as a means of taking pressure off the Poor Law.[31]

The dole could not be financed by the Poor Law and the first intention was to provide on a temporary basis from the NIS funds. In the face of mass unemployment after 1920 this was not possible since income from contributions was inadequate to cover outgoings. The shortfall was presented to the public as a deficit in NIS funds and this became a matter for media and public attention. From the start the dole was regarded as relatively generous and expensive and, inevitably, there were demands that unemployment relief should be placed on a sound insurance basis. At the same time, the dole made the NIS provisions seem niggardly and unduly restrictive. Higher rates were paid from 1919 and the maximum benefit period was extended to twenty-six weeks in 1921. In 1920 the scheme was extended to cover most workers apart from farm labourers, domestic servants, the armed forces, the self-employed and those earning over £250 per annum. In 1921 dependants' (wives and children) allowances were introduced. By the beginning of the 1920s, therefore, the state, through the NIS, was assuming responsibility for most of the unemployed, at least during the early weeks of unemployment. Nevertheless, there was continuing concern about those unemployed workers who had exhausted or were not covered by NIS entitlements. This concern came in part from the Poor Law authorities and was much enhanced with the arrival of heavy unemployment in 1921. The military 'out-of-work donation' continued until December 1921, and new legislation in December 1920 renewed and extended the civilian dole. From this time there was continuous provision throughout the interwar years of the dole under a variety of names – all of these implied a lack of insurance entitlement. In 1921 the dole became 'uncovenanted benefit' which could be paid for sixteen weeks (later increased to twenty-two) in any one year to those who could prove twenty weeks' employment in an insured trade since 1919. In effect, this meant that the state was assuming responsibility for most of the long-term unemployed and, again, the object was to remove pressure from the Poor Law and to avoid the unpopularity of pauperizing significant sections of the working class. As Deacon has shown, this improvement in provision for the unemployed was accompanied by strict application in detail to eliminate scroungers and to reduce the stubborn number of claimants. Since the dole was seen from the start as an alternative to the Poor Law it almost inevitably acquired some of the latter's characteristics. A destitution criterion was applied and this explains some of the complexity. Single people living with their parents and married women were denied benefits unless they could establish lack of support. However, adult males were not means tested until 1931. In the 1920s, therefore, the dole represented a complex mixture of old and new concepts about social security. Controversy also arose because the dole, although below the least generous poverty line, cut into the bottom end of the wage spectrum and a small proportion of applicants, usually unskilled labourers with large families, were better off on the dole than in employment. Unlike the dole, wages were not calculated on a needs basis.

In 1924 the dole was renamed 'Extended Benefit' and could be paid for unlimited periods to those normally in insured employment. In effect, this meant benefits as-of-right for previously insured workers and represented a generous measure by the first Labour Government. Under the Conservatives administrative provisions were tightened and the granting of benefits became more discretionary, in particular, with more vigorous use of the 'not genuinely seeking work' clause which was used to deny benefit in many cases. Alan Deacon has shown how the 'search for the scrounger' became something of a public and bureaucratic obsession during the 1920s. In 1925 in an atmosphere of continuing controversy about unemployment benefits, the Blanesburgh Committee was appointed. Its recommendations were incorporated in legislation in 1927 which turned the dole into 'Transitional Benefits', payable for one year under stricter conditions to those unable to satisfy the requirements for NIS benefits.

The second Labour Government established the Morris Committee in 1929 to investigate procedures and conditions for the payment of the dole. The resulting recommendations were introduced in 1930 and included the abolition of the 'not genuinely seeking work' clause. Also, benefits became more generous and conditions for receiving them were made less strict. Within six months the numbers drawing transitional benefit doubled, rising to 300,000. Although unemployment was rising most of this increase resulted from the changes in the system. With the growing deficit on the Unemployment Fund the level of unemployment benefit became the central feature of an intense debate about public finance which culminated in the fall of the Government. In retrospect, we know that the debt represented a transfer payment which may have benefited the economy by raising the average propensity to consume at a time when demand was constrained. Also, this item was a relatively small part of the public account – being about 7 per cent of total public spending in 1931. Nevertheless, the rate of increase was alarming and this provided a tempting opportunity for the forces of reaction and financial orthodoxy. During the financial crisis of 1931 the Unemployment Fund gained the main attention and was the main item for public expenditure cuts instanced by the May Committee. Following the 1931 crisis the National Government converted the dole into a direct charge on the Treasury and the issue of funding became less controversial.

The Holman–Gregory Committee, which had been appointed in 1930, recommended reductions in benefits, less generous provisions and higher NIS contributions, as well as the introduction of the Family Means Test. The National Government implemented these recommendations in September 1931, and a further economy measure was included in the so-called 'Anomalies Regulations' which had the effect of denying benefit to many married women by ignoring NIS contributions made before marriage. The implicit assumption was that women left the workforce on marriage and the effect was to remove large numbers from the unemployment register. Also, those applying for the dole were means tested by the local Poor Law authorities who operated differing relief scales and applied a household means test which took into account savings and the income of the entire household. As a result, the income of relatives and even lodgers might be deducted from benefits. This removed large numbers from benefit and gave rise to widespread resentment and a flood of complaints which the NUWM attempted to orchestrate. Many authorities applied the means test harshly but in some Labour-controlled areas there was a degree of 'generosity' which caused much concern in Whitehall. In October 1932, Rotherham Public Assistance Committee was replaced by a government commissioner and this marked the beginning of a determined disciplinary exercise. A NUWM march of protest against the means test was met with strong police violence in London but protests against the system continued.

In its final report in 1932 the Holman–Gregory Committee recommended the establishment of an Unemployment Assistance Board (UAB) which would implement a new national scheme. Under legislation introduced in 1934 the UAB was to take over transitional benefits from the Public Assistance Committees (PACs), applying a national means test and paying uniform scales of benefit. In January 1935, the UAB assumed responsibility for 0.8 million recipients of transitional benefit and this precipitated one of the most remarkable public protests of the 1930s. The new rules and scales resulted in widespread disqualifications and reductions in benefits and this gave rise to large-scale protests, especially in areas of heavy unemployment, such as south Wales. There was a rapid government retreat, known as the 'Standstill'. Under this, previous rates of benefit, where higher, were allowed to remain. During the later 1930s there was a gradual progression towards national scales which were more generous than originally intended.

In 1937 the UAB also assumed responsibility for 0.2 million 'able-bodied' poor from the PACs and it could be said that this, in effect, was the end of the unemployment aspect of the Poor Law. The system lingered on until the late 1930s despite the clear acceptance by government in the early 1920s that the Poor Law could not cope with the new pattern of unemployment. Nevertheless, it remained as the last resort until 1937. In interwar circumstances the principle of less eligibility could not be applied and local rates were inadequate as a means of financing unemployment relief. Governments were reluctant to subsidize local Boards of Guardians because they could not be sure of being able to control them and doubted their competence. Also, there were undoubted dangers in fuelling popular protest by forcing people onto the Poor Law. Ironically, in spite of the Poor Law's harsh reputation and the fears that local sources of finance could not cope with heavy unemployment, many Boards were accused of being excessively generous and this manifestation became known as 'Poplarism'. In 1920 the local authority in the London Borough of Poplar, in the docklands area of east London, had refused to pay its rates contribution to the London County Council (LCC). Poplar, as a poor working-class district, had heavy outgoings on poor relief and these were enhanced by relatively generous provisions. The Poplar civic leaders, headed by George Lansbury, later leader of the Labour Party, demanded that richer areas of London should share the costs of poor relief. After a spirited campaign, during which Poplar councillors were imprisoned for defying the High Court, the cost of poor relief was made uniform throughout the LCC area. This politicization of the Poor Law was, of course, a factor in its demise.

By the end of the 1930s national insurance had been firmly established for the majority of the workforce and as the main means of dealing with unemployment. The Poor Law, at least for the 'able-bodied', had finally been abolished and a national system of social security had been established. This administrative structure of support for the unemployed under the NIS and the UAB has, in essence, continued to the present day and should be seen as the central feature in the development of British social policy. Under the Beveridge system of the 1940s the NIS was retained and enhanced and continued as the main provision. The UAB, also enhanced, was renamed the National Assistance Board and the dole of the interwar years is directly traceable to present-day Income Support. National assistance or supplementary benefit remained as the final resort for those who exhausted or were not covered by the NIS and its role became and has remained much more important than Beveridge intended. Indeed, he had assumed that, in the absence of mass unemployment, the UAB would eventually become redundant.

It is difficult to assess the real importance of the new social security system established in Britain, in its essentials, by the early 1920s. Undoubtedly it formed part of a process of political compromise, as well as being, in itself, part of the apparatus of social control. The unemployed were compelled to subject themselves to daily attendance at Labour Exchanges to 'sign on'; benefits were awarded or withdrawn under the petty regulations of a burgeoning bureaucracy and there was always the fear of what would happen if payments ceased. As Alan Deacon has shown, people were much more likely and willing to protest about perceived deficiencies in the payment of unemployment benefits than against unemployment itself.[32] Also, the establishment of the new system appears to coincide with the failure of wages to adjust to levels of unemployment and this is a question of central importance for economic policy. It appears that, in a situation of mass unemployment, social security prevented the wage structure from being undermined by desperation.

VI

Full Employment

'. . . in economics and social sciences, a very important source, often cumulative, of weakness and inadequacy (unlike, usually, in the natural sciences) consists of changes in historical conditions and institutions. Such changes both give rise to new weaknesses and inadequacies and magnify old ones, by creating empirical anomalies or irrelevances in once more acceptable "orthodox" doctrines.'   *T. W. Hutchison, 1981*

'. . . the single most important step towards reducing union influence would be to avoid the inflationary financial policies undertaken in the name of full employment.'   *Samuel Brittan, 1975*

The impact of war

It is often claimed that war brought full employment, although strictly speaking this is not correct. Unemployment was evident until late 1940. During the 1939–45 conflict the British civilian workforce actually fell slightly. The enrolment of 4.5 million people into the armed forces left a chronic labour shortage from the beginning of 1941 as the war effort gathered momentum. In wartime circumstances the urgent necessity was for production at all costs and the usual strictures about containing public spending became less relevant along with concern about inflation and the balance of payments. The influence of the City and the Treasury waned and from 1941 there is clear evidence of a strong Keynesian influence on the management of the war economy. In 1939 Keynes had published *How to Pay for the War* which combined the lessons learned from the First World War with the new principles set out in his *General Theory*. One of the main aims was to avoid inflation through the exercise of new powers and controls including price controls. Purchasing power and inflation were restrained by heavy taxation. Despite recent criticisms of the British wartime achievement, economic management during the Second World War must still be seen as remarkably successful in the circumstances. Alan Booth has argued:[1] 'Wartime policy demonstrated that deficit finance could be so managed to give very full employment *without accelerating inflation* over a substantial period.' Since it is often argued nowadays that this cannot be done, it is worth giving some attention to wartime circumstances.

The war was funded more by taxation than domestic borrowing and this restrained purchasing by higher income groups in particular. Wage demands may have been restrained by an ethos of 'fair shares' which included rationing, conscription and notions of a need for general sacrifice. Ernest Bevin's role as Minister for Labour has been stressed, probably correctly, as an additional factor helping to generate trust, co-operation and a mood of partnership with government in trade union circles. The incorporation of trade unions into wartime economic management was an essential part of government effort to restrain 'cost push' inflation, complementing the fiscal influence on 'demand pull' factors. This was achieved without formal wage control and with a continuance of free collective bargaining. According to a recent commentator, Russell Jones,[2] 'policy makers and academics in general were shown how wage restraint and a not inconsiderable degree of industrial peace had been achieved within the general context of a continuation and extension of prewar bargaining machinery, price and profit control and social reform.'

Although there appears to have been some fall in living standards and most people were probably not fooled by the bogus price index used for propaganda purposes, the reduction was, in the circumstances, slight and acceptable. Above all there was official attention and concern for the supply and cost of basic human needs such as food, shelter and clothing and price control in these areas formed part of the understanding with trade unions. Although wage control was considered, it was not used and proved to be unnecessary.

Wartime circumstances proved to be conducive to several

developments which had been anticipated during the interwar period, and full employment was one of these.[3] Historians will continue to debate the precise influence of war but, at the very least, it accelerated the pace of change. In particular, the war helped to change opinions and provided opportunities for reformers and visionaries such as Keynes and Beveridge. The Beveridge Report of 1942 provided the guiding blueprint for the welfare state and helped to establish a general feeling that after the war things would be different. Although both the Treasury and the Prime Minister appear to have been opposed to the Beveridge proposals they were nudged by the pressure of public opinion towards acceptance in some form. Thus, at a relatively early stage in the war there was a commitment to what appeared to be radical postwar change. One of the basic assumptions in the Beveridge plan was that there would not be a return to the relatively high prewar levels of unemployment and that an average of no more than 8.5 per cent could be maintained for the insured workforce. Unless lower levels of unemployment could be established it would be impossible to fund the Welfare State and, once again, public finance would be strained by the flow of funds into unemployment benefits. It is not surprising, therefore, that Beveridge turned his main attention once again to the question of employment.[4]

The Government had already begun to give some attention to postwar employment, both in general terms and in relation to the financing of welfare payments, before Beveridge announced his full employment enquiry.[5] Apprehension in Whitehall over the prospect of a second Beveridge Report dealing with the employment question provided the impetus for a government white paper on the subject. In 1941 the Treasury had begun to discuss postwar economic management. The initiative in this passed to the Economic Policy Section, led by academic economists recruited for wartime purposes, and to James Meade in particular. Later an Interdepartmental Committee on Post-War Economic Problems was established and a series of papers produced. The white paper on employment policy which was finally published in 1944 has been seen as an historic turning point in economic policy whereby future

British governments were committed to a policy of 'full employment'. The reality is less dramatic and more complex.

Any such commitment could have had no constitutional validity
whatsoever and, although the white paper was issued by a coalition
government, there was no formal commitment at the time by the
political parties which formed the coalition. Several Whitehall
departments, groups and individuals contributed to the draft of the
paper. The Treasury influence was cautious and, on balance,
negative, while the Economic Policy Section provided an optimistic
and essentially Keynesian contribution. It is not surprising, therefore, that the end result was a weak and vague compromise. In Alan
Booth's words:[6] 'It is difficult to avoid the view that the white paper
was a pusillanimous document aimed primarily, though probably
subconsciously, at reducing the pressure on politicians to make
extravagant postwar promises.' In fact, there was no commitment
to anything resembling 'full employment': simply a vague and
qualified hope that government would be able to ensure 'the
maintenance of a high and stable level of employment after the
war'.[7] At the time Britain's balance of payments had deteriorated
alarmingly and postwar prospects appeared to be extremely bleak.
British trade recovery must have appeared a difficult task in a
postwar world of devastation and United States dominance.
Britain's trade links with the Commonwealth were also threatened.
Quite apart from these external problems there were internal
concerns about restraining inflation and maintaining and improving
the efficiency of manufacturing industry.

The caution of Whitehall and the Treasury in particular is not
difficult to understand. Behind the immediate objections was the
fear that Britain was well on the road to becoming a command
economy. However, the white paper did contain elements which
suggested a means of avoiding this while enabling the economy to
be controlled in new ways.[8] It was these aspects which captured
public attention and were used by Aneurin Bevan, Hugh Dalton and
other politicians. Public opinion had made the Beveridge Report
unrejectable and the same force created a full employment policy
where this was probably not intended. As Alan Booth has said:[9]

'The force of public opinion, thus, compelled ministers to treat the very equivocal pledges of the white paper's draftsmen as unambiguous promises of full employment. The force of this emotional commitment helped create the myth that the white paper was the cornerstone of a new postwar order.'

The final step in the creation of the myth that British governments had accepted a formal commitment to promote and maintain full employment came with the rejection of Churchill and the election, with a massive majority, of a Labour Government in 1945. The Conservatives, even under Churchill, were identified as the party of unemployment after the interwar experience. Without this dramatic political change wartime commitments and policy initiatives might not have come to fruition. The lessons of Lloyd George had not been forgotten and, once again, the experiences of the First World War had exerted an influence.

Peace and prosperity

During the era of full employment which lasted from the 1940s until the 1970s governments were usually concerned to reduce rather than to raise the level of demand. In other words, the problem was not maintaining full employment but rather to prevent buoyant demand from creating inflation and balance of payments problems.[10] Although there were occasional boosts given to demand, especially in pre-election periods, and these tended to increase in magnitude and to decline in effectiveness over time, full employment did not usually result from direct government intervention in the economy. Where governments did intervene the adjustments were marginal, raising or lowering unemployment by one percentage point at the most. This makes it obvious that the causes of full employment were real rather than policy-induced, although this should not be taken to imply that government attitudes and policies had no influence. It is more than likely that the buoyancy of postwar investment owed much to the knowledge that the authorities would not allow general depression to emerge without taking remedial action and to the belief that such action would be effective.

The reasons for postwar full employment are not entirely clear but in all industrial nations the mass unemployment of the 1930s did not reappear after the reconstruction phase. After two decades of war and depression there was a good deal of catching up to be done as well as a range of new technologies to introduce and develop. Growth was greatly assisted by new policies of international co-operation promoted by the United States which had emerged in a dominant position. Ironically, American unemployment remained at higher levels than in most European countries until the 1960s. In almost all countries governments became major employers and began to play a more active role in economic management. The establishment of the International Monetary Fund (IMF) and the Bretton Woods system provided a new means of regulating international finance which permitted adjustments but, at the same time, provided stability and induced confidence. In trade the General Agreement on Tariffs and Trade (GATT) provided a set of rules which were designed to eliminate discrimination as well as reducing trade barriers. For a time these institutions proved to be remarkably successful despite British apprehensions. American aid, both in 1945 and later under the Marshall Aid programme, facilitated reconstruction in conditions of full employment. In the three decades after the end of the war individual countries experienced fluctuating economic fortunes but there was no general or international recession. On a world scale there was a sustained investment boom. It was not until 1974 that the cycle became internationally synchronized.

In the immediate postwar period wartime controls, both financial and direct, had to be continued, not least because of severe inflationary pressures and chronic balance of payments weakness.[11] As Chancellor, Dalton adopted a 'cheap money' policy which meant that financial management through interest rate manipulation was not possible and this made controls all the more essential. Under Dalton there was always at least the possibility that wartime controls would pave the way towards peacetime planning in some form. Dalton's downfall in 1947 removed even this remote possibility. The Labour administration was true to the pursuit of its immediate goals of raising output, investment and exports as well as maintaining full employment. However, it lacked any clear longer

term strategy for the economy. In the first years of peace employment, exports and output exceeded expectations. Despite this,
confidence was undermined by the poor balance of payments and
the fuel crisis of 1947 which helped to restore the Treasury to a
position of control over policy. In the buoyant postwar atmosphere
entrepreneurs believed that controls restricted profitability and there
was increasing pressure for removal. This was cleverly communi-
cated to the general public which was anxious for the removal of
rationing and other measures of wartime austerity. For its part, the
Government seems to have seen its nationalization programme as an
alternative to economic control and industrial planning. By the late
1940s British industry had generated a major export revival in
buoyant world markets in the absence of Japanese and German
competition. For a short period at the end of the 1940s Britain
regained the share of world trade it had commanded in 1913. In
these circumstances, government intervention in industry was
resented and resisted and seemed less necessary.

The Labour Government failed to grasp the opportunity of
developing an economic planning programme for postwar Britain
and for British industry in particular. The reasons for this failure
reflect, in part, the nature of the Labour movement and the Labour
Government as well as the pressure of circumstances. Any move
towards planning must inevitably have involved some form of wage
control which seemed to imply conflict with the trade union
movement, in addition to conflict with the business and financial
communities. In the circumstances, a market solution provided the
line of least resistance. However, the essential cornerstone in the
postwar consensus was Keynesian demand management which
appeared to reconcile the private enterprise system with the new
social welfarist aspirations.

Seeking a market solution at the microeconomic level did not
imply a free market. Import licensing continued and market-sharing
arrangements were not attacked until the later 1950s. The softer
markets of the empire and Commonwealth continued to appeal to
British business and preferential tariffs survived the war. While
government, on the whole, chose not to regulate private industry,

industry regulated itself. Since the late nineteenth century British industry had exhibited a strong preference for collusion rather than competition. This had gathered momentum during the interwar years and in the postwar period British industrial inefficiencies relative to other major industrial nations continued. This was reflected in relatively low rates of investment, a poor comparative record in research and development, lagging technology and bad organization at plant and company level. British industry relied upon sheltered, protected and organized markets at home and abroad and became relatively inefficient in doing so. As the international environment became more competitive Britain's export share inevitably declined.

Postwar economic policy
By the late 1940s the new confidence in Keynesian economics convinced most of the British Labour movement that full employment could be maintained without wartime controls or a planning regime. Planning to some minds conveyed notions of Soviet and fascist dictatorships and these models were repugnant. Beveridge had emphasized in 1944 that full employment was possible in a 'free society' but the system which he had in mind involved extensive government regulation of the economy, industry and the labour market.[12] By the end of the 1940s it was widely accepted that such detailed regulation was not required. Less *dirigiste* forms of planning were not seriously considered although other industrial countries turned in this direction. The postwar consensus was based upon a powerful assertion of vested interests by business and trade unions together with a new perception of policy possibilities. By the late 1940s it was generally accepted that a market solution need not restore the chronic unemployment of the interwar years. When the Conservatives assumed office in 1951 they removed most of the remaining controls and what was left of rationing, but in all its main essentials they accepted the new consensus including full employment and the Welfare State.

The postwar consensus had three basic elements. The acceptance of a governmental role and responsibility in controlling the levels of economic activity. The market remained the main mechanism for allocating resources and determining income and wealth in a private enterprise system. Important services such as health and education were to be allocated on a needs basis rather than being left to the market. This consensus was far from being totally clear and universally accepted. Major areas of conflict between the political parties arose, in particular, over private property issues including nationalization and housing and sections of each party pulled in different directions. However, full employment did not arise as an issue for debate and was accepted as a fact of economic and political life.

Between the end of the war and the mid-1960s the average level of unemployment was only 1.8 per cent which involved about 400,000 individuals. In most years demand restraint rather than stimulation was attempted. Control was asserted through changes in public expenditure and taxation and the balanced budget idea, either annually or over longer periods, was abandoned. To a lesser extent control was also asserted through monetary policies including interest rate manipulation and controls over bank and hire purchase credit. The application of Keynesian techniques to the management of the economy really became established in the 1950s and was dubbed 'fine tuning'. Despite the continuation of full employment and higher and better sustained economic growth, 'fine tuning' was criticized for its nature and timing.[13] It was suggested that intervention came too late, with the result that fluctuations were intensified rather than reduced and downturns in the economy were prolonged. Governments were also criticized in detail on particular aspects of fiscal and monetary policy. Meanwhile, the problem of regional imbalance and relatively heavy unemployment in some parts of the country remained and, in relative terms, became more severe over time. The idea that all economic problems could be solved by expanding or contracting the whole economy remained open to question. Regional unemployment could not be eliminated by reflation which created intense labour shortages and wage inflation in the more prosperous areas and balance of payments problems for the economy as a whole.

Full employment was only one of a number of economic policy objectives. The other main targets were stable prices (or a lower rate of inflation); economic growth; and a viable balance of payments. Achieving all these aims simultaneously was difficult if not impossible. Full employment and growth were not considered to be in conflict, but it was widely believed that a tight labour market was the main cause of inflation which, in turn, threatened the balance of payments. These concerns and trade-offs became central and familiar issues in postwar political economy. From the late 1950s there was less emphasis on full employment and increasing worry about economic growth. This was partly because full employment had been achieved and partly also because it came to be believed that the achievement was economically damaging.

Although in retrospect the first two postwar decades may seem like a golden age, at least in terms of rapid economic growth and full employment, there were considerable misgivings at the time. In particular, these related to Britain's relatively poor growth performance compared with other industrial nations. While British postwar growth was perhaps the most rapid and best sustained in recorded history, other countries were doing much better in terms of economic growth as measured by economists.[14] For Britain this had alarming long-run consequences in terms of comparative living standards. From being the richest nation in Europe in 1950 Britain seemed destined to become one of the poorest.[15] Slow growth was attributed to balance of payments problems which obliged governments to restrain demand which, in turn, reduced growth. When left to itself the economy was capable of growing rapidly but, from time to time, growth had to be checked for balance of payments reasons. This phenomenon became known as 'stop, go'. British economic history over these years is concerned with a series of crises on external account and currency problems. Much attention was given to explaining these problems and the view became established that declining export competitiveness was the main cause. Britain's share of total world exports actually rose above the 1937 level in the late 1940s but then began to decline rapidly as the industrial world recovered from war. By 1970 it was less than half the prewar level.

Clearly there were links between rising wages and rising prices, but the exact nature of these was debatable and complex. There was no clear agreement on whether price increases were caused by rising wages or whether wages simply followed prices. Nevertheless, Keynesian economists were increasingly inclined to adopt the somewhat ironical assertion that if wage-earners acted rationally and attempted to maximize, this would undermine the system. In 1958 a New Zealand economist, A. W. Phillips, published a paper which suggested a long-run systematic link between the annual percentage level of unemployment and the rate of increase in money wage rates in Britain since 1861.[16] Although they appeared to be based upon empirical observation, these findings were controversial and there was a good deal of challenge and attempted revision. Nevertheless, by the early 1960s the systematic relationship which Phillips claimed to have identified became widely accepted. The so-called 'Phillips Curve' became a vogue subject for discussion amongst professional economists. These discussions related mainly to technical questions about interpretations of data and relating data to mathematical expressions. Basically, Phillips was simply saying that the labour market worked in conformity with the economics textbooks so that, at low levels of unemployment, there would be high increases in wages, and vice versa. It followed quite clearly from this approach that wages could be controlled through variations in levels of unemployment. By the early 1960s some economists were beginning openly to urge this. During the 1960s there was increasing acceptance of the view that full employment and price stability were incompatible and there were increasing references to 'overfull' employment and to the 'monopoly power' of trade unions. The latter influence, it was argued, was asserted through the ballot box rather than as a result of the application of industrial muscle. Since governments were committed to full employment this gave trade unions irresistible power to force wages upwards. The fact remains that inflation levels during the 1950s and 1960s were very modest compared with more recent times and usually well below 5 per cent. In the 1980s average levels of inflation have been much higher despite the massive increase in unemployment.

Of course, concern about wages was a very old theme. Wages had been held during the war and under the postwar Labour Government real wages actually fell between 1945 and 1950. In general the trade unions continued their wartime policy of co-operating with the government to restrain increases in return for a continuation of free collective bargaining.[17] This grudging and far from frictionless co-operation set a pattern for postwar Labour administrations which, on the whole, were far more successful in limiting wage increases than Conservative administrations. Ironically, postwar Labour Governments in Britain, without exception, came to see the restraint of working-class incomes as a basic condition of economic and political success. They successfully used their fraternal links with the trade union movement to this end.

Wage concerns were given a greater sense of urgency and relevance by the atmosphere of economic crisis which affected the first Wilson Government elected in 1964. For the first Labour Government in thirteen years it was unthinkable to use unemployment as a means of controlling wages and prices. However, within a few years the Wilson Government was forced into devaluation and this was accompanied by a secular rise in unemployment through which it was hoped resources could be diverted from consumption into investment and exports at a time when world trade was beginning to grow very rapidly. Since the war there had been more or less continuous attempts to restrain wages by non-market means or 'incomes policies'.[18] These ranged from exhortations about the dangers of increase to statutory control. From the 1960s wage control appeared to become both more difficult and more urgent. The tendency for incomes to grow faster than production was increasingly forced into public attention. In its manifesto the Wilson Government had declared: 'Labour's incomes policy will not be unfairly directed at lower paid workers and public employees; instead it will apply in an expanding economy to all incomes; to profits, dividends and rents as well as to wages and salaries.'

The pledge to control non-wage income carried little conviction although it recognized the unreasonableness of an expectation that only wage-earners should avoid maximization. In the 1960s governments were expected to promote a degree of economic and social justice and this was difficult to reconcile with wage control. By 1968, after a period of disillusionment and a forced devaluation of sterling, the Government proposed to reform the collective bargaining process. In part this was a response to the Donovan Commission which had highlighted the informal aspects of British industrial relations and stressed the need to avoid unofficial stoppages as well as strengthening the employer side of negotiations. Early in 1969 a white paper called *In Place of Strife* indicated the Government's intentions and caused a storm within the Labour movement. After intense trade union protests and dissension within the Cabinet the proposals were withdrawn. In its final year the Wilson Government presided over a wage explosion.

By 1970 there was a firmly established view over most of the British political spectrum that the trade unions were causing the country irreparable damage which was reflected in poor economic performance. In fact, the extent to which formal labour organization is to be blamed for wage pressures remains unclear. Trade union leaders frequently led from behind as members demanded that real and relative wages be maintained. In most years the trade union movement was used by government as an instrument of wage restraint. Also, in the 1970s inflation probably resulted more from changes in commodity prices than collective bargaining processes. Nevertheless, the concern about trade union power which had become a major issue in the later 1960s continued. This appeared to be supported by the more prominent economic theories at that time although more thoughtful economists did, occasionally, point to the relative inefficiencies of British industrial organization and management. However, even this could be blamed upon trade union 'obstructiveness' or 'restrictive practices'. There was also growing disillusionment with incomes policies, which seemed destined, at best, to have only short-term success. When the Heath Government came into office in 1970 it proposed to curb trade union power by changing the law as well as making short-term use of incomes policy. The result was a series of bitter confrontations with powerful trade unions, and eventual failure. In 1974 Heath chose to call an election during a miners' strike but failed to obtain the anti-trade union mandate which he sought.

The ending of full employment

Until the late 1960s Britain had full employment with what can only be viewed in hindsight as a very modest rate of inflation. Between 1956 and 1968 the annual rate of price inflation never rose above 5 per cent and was usually much lower. Viewed in these terms the Keynesian orthodoxy seems to have worked with a high degree of success. However, there was increasing concern about Britain's balance of payments weakness and poor (relative) growth performance. The problem did not lie in achieving growth as such since the economy, when left to its own devices, showed strong growth potential. But this tended to create balance of payments problems which were checked by deflation. This, in turn, reduced growth.

The British problem of relative decline was highly complex and has not yet been properly analysed by historians. In retrospect it seems likely that the contemporary obsession with formal trade unions will be seen as largely misguided. Also, it may be concluded that inflation was not the main source of weakness and that, were it not for other factors, it should have been possible to cope with the modest rates of inflation which prevailed before the mid-1970s. It is clear that the British manufacturing system became relatively inefficient, generating poor export performance and high propensity to import – but this may have been the effect rather than cause of poor growth. In 1950 Britain *was* competitive if only because of war destruction elsewhere. Part of the explanation for relative decline lies in what happened elsewhere and it is possible that British resources and circumstances would not have made it possible for Britain to grow as fast as other nations. Most commentators seem to agree that much faster growth could have been achieved in the absence of balance of payments problems. In part at least these problems were a legacy of war as well as a consequence of the attempt to preserve great power status in the postwar world. Also, some of Britain's currency and balance of payments difficulties stemmed from the fact that financial leadership had shifted emphatically to the United States and sterling was no longer the leading reserve currency.

From the second half of the 1960s Britain's economic problems seem to have intensified and the Wilson Government sacrificed most of its programme to a forlorn attempt to avoid devaluation. From 1966 unemployment remained over half a million and it came close to a million in 1972. This increase in unemployment gave rise to debate about meaning and measurement and the process of raising tolerance levels commenced both in Whitehall and elsewhere. It was suggested by some economists that higher benefits had induced more people to become unemployed and that redundancy payments encouraged longer periods between employment.[19] These and other influences were thought to promote 'voluntary' unemployment. Some economists began to suggest that most unemployment was not 'demand deficient' and in the early 1970s these views were taken up by politicians including Keith Joseph and Margaret Thatcher.[20]

In fact, the first departures from the postwar full employment pledge had possibly already taken place under the first Wilson Government in the late 1960s when the exchange rate had been given priority over all else. When the failure to preserve sterling became clear the Government deflated against a rising trend in unemployment in an attempt to make the devaluation effective.

The Heath Government, which came into office in 1970, was resolved under its 'Selsdon' programme to reduce government influence and restore market forces to a dominant role in the economy. Inflation was to be controlled by incomes policy and a tight monetary squeeze while legislation to curb the trade unions was also introduced. Government attempts to halt rising unemployment by modest reflation failed and by 1972 the official figure reached 900,000. The politically sensitive figure of 1 million unemployed began to seem likely and this was generally regarded as being unacceptable. In this situation the Heath Government resolved to give a massive boost to the economy which would cure unemployment and break through the balance of payments impasse simultaneously, taking the economy to a higher growth path. Heath's 'U-turn' in 1972 involved a move to a floating exchange rate combined with rapid economic expansion. This episode, sometimes known as the 'Barber Boom', after the Chancellor who presided over it, has been widely condemned in retrospect and the lesson was not lost on the right wing of the Conservative Party, which was confirmed in its conviction that expansionist policies were disastrous. Similar conclusions were not reached in relation to the failure of Heath's industrial relations policies but important lessons were learned about confrontation with major unions.

The second Wilson Government, which came into office in 1974, inherited sharply escalating wages and prices and a rapidly deteriorating balance of payments – the result in large part of the sharp rise in oil prices in 1973 combined with the Heath–Barber policies. After the 'social contract' had failed to hold wages, and in an atmosphere of severe crisis, Chancellor Denis Healey openly abandoned the postwar full employment policy in his 1975 budget. At this time, unemployment stood at about 900,000, which was just under 4 per cent of the workforce, and there was clearly a strong upward trend. Nevertheless, Healey raised taxes and cut public spending sharply in a manner which would have been unthinkable for previous administrations. Later in the same year the Prime Minister, James Callaghan, explained to a bewildered and bitter Labour Party Conference that Keynesian solutions had become extinct. In the words of Russell Jones,[21] 'the budget of 1975 marks a major benchmark in postwar economic history. It signalled the suspension of the commitment to full employment as it had been known since 1945.' By the time Thatcher came into office in 1979 there was clear precedent for the abandonment of full employment, as it had been known, in the face of major economic and financial emergency, although no previous government had resorted to mass unemployment as a primary tool of policy. Future historians may wish to ask if the crisis of the mid-1970s might have been met with different policies.

The menace of inflation

Before 1945 in Britain it is necessary to go back to Tudor times in order to find a sustained inflation situation in peacetime. During most of the nineteenth century and through the interwar years the general trend in prices was stable or downwards. Since the Second World War most countries have experienced an unusual degree of inflation and have learned to live with it.

Inflation can be defined as a rise in prices across a wide range of economic activity. Such a rise in the general price level can result from a multiplicity of causes and the well-known definition of 'too much money chasing too few goods' may not always be appropriate. For example, Geoffrey Howe's act, as Chancellor, in raising VAT to 15 per cent had an immediate inflationary effect even though, in the short run, the quantities of money and goods in supply did not change. Similarly, the OPEC decisions which quadrupled world oil prices in 1973–4 were immediately inflationary. In the modern economy there are highly complex mechanisms of price fixing and 'money' can assume many different forms. It may be simplistic, therefore, to suggest that prices are only governed by money supply relative to goods and that there is a simple nexus between the two. Nevertheless, most economists would probably affirm this relationship at least in a long-run context.

Inflation has costs and benefits. It may, in some circumstances, stimulate economic activity and help to overcome economic bottle-necks. During the 1950s and 1960s some economists suggested that a mild degree of inflation could stimulate investment. However, it is also clear that inflation can cause inefficiencies and injustices and that it may become uncontrollable. (Similar arguments also apply to deflation.) During the interwar period, and since, there have been frequent warnings against the danger of hyper-inflation such as that which occurred in Germany and much of central Europe in the early 1920s. However, this took place with a certain amount of official connivance. Hyper-inflation has never been a threat in Britain, at least during the present century. Even in 1975 inflation only reached 27 per cent and this must be seen as a relatively modest figure against the experience of countries such as Israel and Brazil in recent years.

Indeed there are several examples of countries with inflation rates in excess of 100 per cent during the past decade, but without serious danger of collapse.

Inflation came to be seen as a great menace in the 1970s and it was widely suggested to be Britain's number one problem. In the 1980s the defeat of inflation was promulgated as Thatcher's primary aim. It came to be accepted in Britain that inflation was a major evil which had to be banished, if necessary, at considerable economic and social cost. There was also, implicitly, a notion that this could be a once and for all purgative process, and this was a view encouraged by Thatcher who frequently spoke about 'squeezing inflation out of the system'.

Is it self-evident that inflation is an unmitigated evil which has to be defeated at any cost? One way of approaching this question is to ask who suffers from inflation? The answer from the economics textbooks is of course those on fixed incomes. By the late 1970s few such people existed in Britain. Wage and salary earners more than kept pace with rising prices and state pensions and benefits were indexed. The direct victims of inflation were, in fact, a small and dwindling minority with little voice or voting power and, indeed, where serious problems existed, they were soon solved by forms of indexation and other devices.

While it may be hard to find large numbers of individuals, or any significant section of society, suffering directly from inflation, could it be said that society as a whole was threatened? Possibly such a threat could come from a deteriorating balance of payments on current account as inflation priced exports out of overseas markets and sucked in imports. This would only happen, of course, if inflation was significantly higher than in competitor countries and if there were no exchange rate adjustments. In fact, British inflation was not disastrously high compared with competitor nations and there is some evidence that price factors were not the main cause of British export loss. It is possible to argue that Britain's postwar economic difficulties were not, in general, the direct result of inflation. British price increases were not much higher than the average even in the most successful economies and by the 1970s a system of floating exchange rates became established so that exchange rate movements could take account of inflation differentials.

The real fears relating to inflation were much more complex and fundamental to the system. By the 1970s Britain's poor rates of investment and a declining profit share in national income were being highlighted and there was increasing concern about declining profitability although profits were difficult to define and measure. In the interwar years, despite falling prices, there had been a fear of inflation in British ruling circles which verged on paranoia. It was believed that inflation during and just after the First World War had seriously damaged Britain's international economic and financial position and may have helped to undermine British pre-eminence. Some of this inflation had been deliberate in the sense that it flowed from political decisions taken during the war and immediately after. The fear in the Treasury was that in democratic society inflation was a normal temptation for politicians unless the canons of 'sound finance' were asserted. Both the gold standard and the balanced budget were means to this end. At the end of the horror scale there was the example of Germany in the 1920s where government 'irresponsibility' had culminated in currency collapse and the destruction of savings on a massive scale. Some other European countries had similar experiences and provided a convenient warning against even minor departures from financial orthodoxy which was asserted from 1921 and coincided with mass unemployment. Finally, there was the fear that under universal suffrage, with widespread and successful trade union organization, private enterprise could not survive successfully in highly inflationary conditions. Since peacetime inflation usually coincided with a tight labour market and wage-earners more than kept pace with prices, inflation could squeeze profits and deter investment in productive activities. Also, since the supply of most commodities was inflexible in the short run, inflation gave rise to adverse terms of trade, not just for Britain but for the industrial nations in general.

Inflation was seen as a fundamental threat upsetting the balance of power in the entire economic system. This reaction, which was in part instinctive, was evident in Britain throughout the entire interwar period and it seems to have emerged once more in the 1970s. Inflation destroyed savings, profits and wealth. In so far as there was a choice between inflation and unemployment the latter was preferable. It is clear, therefore, that unemployment, far from being an accident or the by-product of crisis, was the chosen solution in both periods. In so far as there was a trade-off between the two, it was decided that unemployment was preferable to inflation. In part this was because unemployment threatened those at the bottom of society most severely while inflation threatened those at the top.

VII

Unemployment and Policy

'It is the orthodox Treasury dogma, steadfastly held, that whatever might be the political or social advantages, very little additional employment can, in fact, and as a general rule, be created by state borrowing and state expenditure.' *Winston Churchill, 1925*

'Let us be quite clear. Let us be absolutely clear. You will not reduce unemployment by increasing what governments spend or borrow.' *Nigel Lawson, 1984*

'It is not sufficiently understood that it simply isn't within the Government's power to determine the level of unemployment.' *Nigel Lawson, 1985*

The role of government

Problems which arise in economic development can be solved in different ways and unemployment is no exception to this. In the world today there is a broad range from command economies to the relatively unrestrained private enterprise systems which operate in the United States and much of Latin America. One of the main issues in contemporary policy discussion is the role of government, with economists urging more or less intervention and analysing the public–private sector divide.

After the Second World War what has sometimes been called 'big government' emerged in most advanced industrial economies and in almost all countries the state assumed responsibility for the running of the economy. There were massive increases in public employment and governments which failed to deliver prosperity and full employment usually lost office. By the 1960s even the American government joined the trend with the advent of the Kennedy administration. Planning regimes emerged in several European countries and Japan achieved considerable economic success through a unique blend of government and business.

This new-found faith in government proved to be short-lived. In the 1970s new circumstances combined with new theories gave rise to a complete reversal of previous policy trends. Economic management had become much more difficult and important areas had slipped beyond public control. An increasing share of production was in the hands of multinational companies which were, to a degree, beyond the control of individual governments; capital markets changed and became more international as accumulated quantities of mobile private funds began to have an important economic impact; economies had become more open, trade had become freer and treaty obligations limited the scope for state control. Also, economic theories began to suggest that governments not only should not, but also could not attempt to control in the general interest. By the 1980s the Thatcher Government in Britain was leading the world in what appeared to be a rout of interventionism. Deregulation, privatization, tax reductions and expenditure cuts became part of an international trend which transcended political boundaries. The vogue was followed with enthusiasm by Labor administrations in Australia and New Zealand and Mikhail Gorbachev's promulgation of *Perestroika* and its effects in eastern Europe were frequently seen as part of the same process. Some would see Reaganomics in the United States as a major exception to this trend. There can be little doubt that heavy government spending and a massive budget deficit did much to reduce American unemployment, although the President attributed these effects to his 'supply-side' measures.

Since the 1930s the world has witnessed a dramatic rise and fall in government economic intervention and this has been accompanied by even more remarkable changes in attitudes and expectations about government economic management. This chapter will be mainly concerned with these changes which have coincided with the rise and fall of full employment.

Classical and new microeconomic arguments suggest that only the economy can create employment and this view is illustrated by frequent Thatcherite references to what is termed 'real jobs'. This view is unrealistic since authority can and often does intervene to reallocate resources. Indeed, authority may be a complete substitute for market systems. Private power also affects the allocation of employment through a range of influences, including employer paternalism and labour market strategies, and the power of organized labour may also play a part. At a deeper level the social and cultural forces which define work, allocate training and education and establish qualifications do much to determine who is employed and in what capacity.

In the early Middle Ages the manorial system allocated occupations on the basis of feudal hierarchy. With the emergence of the modern state in the form of absolute monarchy new forms of organization and state intervention, usually for revenue and defence purposes, followed. By the sixteenth century clear notions about state responsibilities and the 'national interest' were beginning to emerge in the form of mercantilism, which tended to assume that most forms of economic life could be controlled. In Tudor England there was some regulation, or attempted regulation, of wages and employment, for example under the Statute of Artificers. There was also unemployment relief in the form of a Poor Law. It was not until the mid-nineteenth century that the combined emergent influences of classical economics and industrial capitalism swept away the remaining vestiges of mercantilism, promoting what is usually termed *laissez-faire*.

Under this system, first articulated by Adam Smith in the late eighteenth century, state authority was usually confined to basic functions of defence and law and order. In *The Wealth of Nations* (1776) Smith attacked state intervention, other than in a few carefully defined areas, as a pernicious influence which inhibited the creation of wealth. These views have been revived in the 1980s and have gained a readier acceptance than Smith obtained in the late eighteenth century. It was not until the 1840s that Victorian Britain moved emphatically to *laissez-faire* through the acceptance of free trade, its most central feature. With the emergence of industrial capitalism the new philosophy triumphed and was underpinned by

'Victorian values' which emphasized the individualistic virtues of thrift, hard work and self-help.

The new industrial middle class was represented by the Liberal Party and *laissez-faire* philosophy was epitomised by one leading politician, in particular. As Chancellor, W. E. Gladstone reduced income tax to 2 old pence (0.8p) in the pound and hoped to abolish it. Minimizing state intervention, taxation and expenditure was a nineteenth-century Liberal philosophy which was adopted and partially implemented by Thatcherite Conservatives in the 1980s. Hence the frequent suggestion that Thatcher is at odds with Tory tradition, which has an interventionist and paternalistic aspect.

In the years up to 1914 British governments did not attempt economic management in the modern sense, because of limited revenue and regulatory powers. Between the 1880s and 1914 policies for unemployment developed within the severe constraints imposed by middle-class public opinion which favoured a low tax regime. As a result of the First World War there were dramatic changes in government power, in the revenue base, and in perceptions of the role of the state. After 1918 Britain began to function as a modern democracy for the first time with women and excluded sections of working-class men exercising the vote. With the new Labour Party constitution of 1918 it was clear that the labour movement was beginning to see the state as a potential means of working-class advancement. Meanwhile, sections of business also had new perceptions, seeing government emerging as a major customer and a potential bestower of tariff protection and other forms of assistance.

Economic policy in the interwar period
The interwar years saw a partial transition from *laissez-faire* to the modern managed economy.[1] For a time after the First World War orthodox finance was abandoned, in part because of fears about political stability. Against a background of inflation, rising unit costs and depreciating exchange, the Treasury and the Bank of England began to urge retrenchment through reduced money supply and a restoration of the gold standard as soon as possible.[2] In

1920 interest rates were increased sharply and there were cuts in public borrowing and spending under the 'Geddes Axe'. There are grounds for comparing the downturn at the beginning of the 1920s with that at the beginning of the 1980s. In both episodes there were severe cutbacks in government spending in selected areas, sharp increases in real interest rates to curb inflation and rising currency values which damaged exports. In the early 1920s unemployment rose to alarming levels with a massive shake-out of labour in manufacturing. Employers were able to take advantage of this situation in eliminating less efficient manpower and operations, and restoring the 'right to manage'. The result was higher unemployment and productivity improvement.

In the 1920s full employment was sacrificed in an attempt to restore Britain's international economic role. In essence this meant restoring competitiveness through reduced wage costs, and unemployment had a clear role in this process. A restored gold standard was central to the aim of re-establishing the pre-1914 financial structure. Since devaluation was not considered, price reductions were a necessary preliminary to a return to gold by Britain. In 1925 Winston Churchill as Chancellor, with the almost unanimous support of expert opinion apart from Keynes, took the decision to return to gold. It is generally agreed that sterling was overvalued by about 10 per cent (against the United States dollar) and that this was harmful to exports and caused unemployment. However, the major damage which resulted from gold standard policy in the 1920s was a decade of deflation and dear money in a vain attempt to restore prewar parity and the prewar system.[3]

The 1920s ended with world depression and attempts at international economic co-operation failed. In the 1930s economic policies became narrow and nationalistic with increasing tariff and other trade barriers, competitive devaluations and trade diversion. With the enforced departure from gold in 1931 sterling became a managed currency and this made 'cheap money' possible. In 1931-2 free trade was finally abandoned and protection with empire preference introduced. In a world of restricted and contracting trade Britain as a major trader was especially vulnerable and this was

reflected in lagging exports during the 1930s with obvious consequences for employment in the export industries.

British industry in the interwar years failed to take full advantage
of the gains new technology and methods of organization offered.
By the end of the 1920s the United States had established a massive
lead in industrial productivity. In part this may be attributed to
British exporting difficulties, but market failure and conservative
attitudes provide a more fundamental explanation. British managers
appear to have preferred collusion and market-sharing to competition.[4] One answer to adversity was 'rationalization' which began
with voluntary schemes in the 1920s and was followed by compulsory schemes in the 1930s. The aim was to reduce capacity and, in
the process, jobs were destroyed. In the long run there was the hope
that a more efficient economy would emerge. Clearly there were
many signs of a reduced faith in the market which had been dear to
the nineteenth-century liberal philosophy. There was a drift towards greater concentration, reduced competition, tariff protection,
collusion, market control and manipulation and much of this was
with government connivance. Meanwhile the 'planning movement'
of the 1930s, supported by Harold Macmillan and others and
ranging across the political spectrum, neglected to consider detailed
industrial planning and failed to grasp the opportunities on offer.[5]
There were important relaxations from classical economic orthodoxy in the 1930s and it may be wrong to assume that the
Government was hidebound by classical economic dogma. The
adoption of protection and empire preference in 1931–2 was a major
turning point in principle. The 'cheap money' opportunity was
seized very quickly in 1932. From 1934 there were relaxations in the
balanced budget dogma and these were intensified in order to
respond to the need for rearmament. During the rearmament
programme in the later 1930s attention was given to regional
considerations and this was possible since a number of traditional
and depressed industries were involved. Jobs were created as a result
and this indicated the potential for interventionary measures. It has
been claimed that 1930s rearmament created a million jobs.[6]

In recent years there has been a major reassessment of British economic policy during the interwar years, much of it informed by access to state papers in the Public Records Office. Also, empirical historical research and new economic methods and theory have led to new conclusions about policy effectiveness and alternatives. The belief in a simple Keynesian solution, frustrated by classical economic dogma in the Treasury and elsewhere, has to be rejected. Few people now challenge the view that multipliers were low and especially regional multipliers in the depressed areas.[7] Thus the unemployment-reducing potential of demand stimulation was limited. Also, any attempt by government to stimulate the economy would have encountered difficulties with exchange rates, the balance of payments and financial markets. Interwar notions of 'crowding out' appear to be rather more robust than before and the 'rational expectations' hypothesis may have given the 'Treasury view' a new lease of life.[8]

Many interwar policy pronouncements have re-emerged in similar forms since 1979. In 1929 the Treasury issued a white paper on employment policy which contained an approach which Nigel Lawson and John Major would find acceptable today.[9] Although the economic jargon differs the essence and real effects of policy are remarkably similar. In both the 1920s and the 1980s it is possible to defend policies in logical theoretical terms while showing that such policies did not and could not have succeeded in solving the unemployment problem.

The Keynesian revolution

The 'Keynesian revolution' is an important area of on-going academic research and discussion. Keynes was both a complex character and a prolific writer.[10] As with Marx and other great thinkers, his views are open to different interpretations and have generated different lines of intellectual development. By the 1950s a version of Keynesian economics had been integrated into what was essentially a classical framework developed by Hicks, Pigou and Modigliani and propagated by Samuelson and other writers of new economics texts.[11] The so-called 'neo-classical synthesis' presented Keynesian views in a static equilibrium framework and this version was extremely vulnerable to the monetarist assault which commenced in the late 1960s. If Keynes had lived and remained active longer it is possible that developments might have been different. He might have opposed the 'neo-classical synthesis' and the eventual reassertion of a concept of long-run equilibrium as the central principle of economics, although it must be said that he showed few signs of doing so in his final years. Keynes was often ambiguous and his economic thought and personality contained a fundamental contradiction: on the one hand he was a Liberal Party member with an emotional commitment to nineteenth-century liberalism; on the other, he had little faith in the free market as a route to social success. The essence of his approach to political economy was an attempt to reconcile these contradictions. Hopes that Keynes might have produced a complete alternative to classical economics were doomed to disappointment. The work of Patinkin completed the 'neo-classical synthesis' and the Keynesian system became merely a special case in what was essentially a classical system. Although Keynes appeared to have called into question the basic classical idea of market equilibrium, attempts by Leijonhufvud and Clower to restore a disequilibrium approach to economics failed to command support.[12] Although economists at Cambridge, in particular Joan Robinson, Kaldor and Kahn, continued to expound purer and less classical versions of Keynesianism, these commanded respect rather than commitment from academics and economics continued to be taught as an equilibrium system with the classical structures remaining intact.

The end of the Keynesian era

Until the late 1960s Britain had full employment with what, in retrospect, can only be regarded as a very modest rate of inflation. From the late 1960s faith in the traditional Keynesian remedies began to be undermined by circumstances and this coincided with an intellectual attack upon the Keynesian approach headed by Milton Friedman. The new approach was labelled 'monetarist' but other titles emerged including 'new classical', 'neo-classical', 'new microeconomic' and 'market economics'. These will be used interchangeably to make points of emphasis. The critics argued that Keynesian economics had had a superficial and temporary success but that this concealed underlying problems which, in the long run, surfaced and became critical in the form of inflation and unemployment. Indeed, that Keynesian policies made these problems worse than they might have been. From the 1960s it appeared that expansionary measures were less effective in raising employment levels; instead they appeared to accelerate inflation. Indeed, by 1976 James Callaghan was telling the Labour Party, 'It used to be thought that a nation could just spend its way out of a recession and increase employment by cutting taxes and boosting government spending. I tell you in all candour that that option no longer exists.'[13] The simple Keynesian remedy was being rejected.

There were two basic aspects to what was termed monetarism. Firstly, the belief that it was the quantity of money (variously defined) in circulation which determined price levels and that inflation was the result of excessive money supply. Secondly, there was a new-found faith in the free market mechanism and a reassertion of classical economic views in a real world context (see Chapter III). Monetarism was generally regarded as an eccentric theoretical cult until the late 1960s when it began to be taken seriously. This owed much to Milton Friedman, whose personality and writing established the new doctrine. However, circumstances also played a major part since by this time there appeared to be a desperate need to find some escape from the menace of inflation. The occurrence, simultaneously, of high inflation and high unemployment appeared to negate the basic Keynesian wisdom, while Keynesians seemed only to be able to advocate endless wage control, which tended to be ephemeral and ineffective. Controlling money supply offered a new panacea. There was also a blissful coincidence between what the new economics advocated and traditional political views on the right of the spectrum which asserted individualism and anti-government attitudes. Reducing state influence and intervention, cutting taxes and public spending, weakening the power of organized labour, sound money, deregulation, privatization and other proposals had considerable appeal for some of the most privileged and influential sectors of society. They also appealed to new middle-income groups in private employment who failed to see much benefit from state welfare and redistribution and progressive taxation. To many the new economics had a simple logic which appealed to non-economists and to the financial community in particular. Keynesian economists were divided and in some disarray. They failed to provide an effective intellectual counter-attack and many flirted with the new approach.[14]

The economic difficulties of the 1970s provided a fertile seedbed for the new economics which owed so much to one man in particular. Milton Friedman, the child of poor Jewish immigrants, was born in New York in 1912. By the mid-1950s Friedman had begun to acquire an international reputation, albeit as an eccentric economist outside the mainline Keynesian orthodoxy. With the help of others at Chicago Friedman reformulated and revived the quantity theory of money and attracted mild but sceptical interest from the economics profession. Friedman's major intellectual breakthrough came from the testing of historical data using statistical and econometric methods. His major work, with Anna Schwarz, was *A Monetary History of the United States*, published in 1963. This massive study of economic history sought to show that in the United States between 1867 and 1960 there had been a clear relationship between changes in economic activity and money stock and that this relationship was stable. The work also sought to establish that changes in money stock did not simply result from changes in economic activity but, on the contrary, were the major influence on the economy. American depressions, including the major downturn of 1929, were explained in terms of monetary contractions. Friedman sought to establish a clear and stable link between money growth and income.

In 1967 Friedman was elected president of the American Economic Association and in the following year, in his presidential address, he attacked and revised the Phillips Curve and presented the 'natural rate of unemployment' concept which most economists now accept. By this time, as the world began to confront increasingly severe problems of inflation, his views appeared to have a particular relevance. In the 1970s they began to replace the Keynesian orthodoxy.

Although Friedman must be given most of the credit for pioneering the new classical approach, a new wave of American economists including Lucas, Sargent, Barro and many others, sometimes known as the 'Young Fogeys', have carried the momentum since the 1970s. Their work combined 'intellectual brilliance, logical rigour and apparent policy relevance'[15] and represented the most important development in economic theory since Keynes. Friedman had suggested that it was possible for governments to reduce the level of unemployment below the 'natural rate', temporarily, but that this would accelerate inflation and might lead to higher unemployment in the long run.[16] The new classicals reasserted the traditional classical view that levels of output and employment were determined by real market influences, so that money variables including the quantity of money and government expenditure could only influence prices. Friedman's theory of 'adaptive expectations', which suggested that the market anticipated price changes on the basis of previous experience, left open the possibility of a role for government, albeit a risky one. The new theory of 'rational expectations' suggested that the market would adjust its expectations to a change in government policy on the basis of the most informed concepts so that reflation would be ineffective. Thus it was argued that governments not only should not but also could not influence the level of unemployment. Any attempt to raise employment above the 'natural rate' would immediately be translated into inflation. Thus the new school were arguing that the market worked quickly and effectively in accordance with classical theory. The implications for public policy were dramatic: there was no role for government and any attempt to assert one was positively harmful.[17]

The new classical approach was based ultimately on the work of Walras, who, in the 1870s, had established a pure theory of general market equilibrium. Markets moved towards equilibrium through price signals and mechanisms, or what Walras called 'tatonnement', and simultaneous equilibrium in all markets was possible. Equilibrium was reached when supply exactly matched demand and markets cleared. The Walrasian system assumed perfect markets and an absence of institutions such as government or trade unions.[18] Nevertheless, the new classical school managed to establish the view that the real world could be analysed in terms of mathematical market models derived, essentially, from Walras. They suggested that in the real world output and employment would operate at equilibrium levels and deviations would only occur when prices differed from what had been anticipated. Any tight definition of 'full employment' was likely to be above the 'natural rate' and, therefore, inflationary. It followed that government attempts to maintain employment at a level above that dictated by the market were harmful, inflationary and likely to lead in the long run to even higher levels of unemployment. An even stronger case against government intervention could be made by using the notion of 'crowding out'. This together with other classical economic views suggested that if government increased taxes this cut real incomes and damaged the economy; if government increased money supply this caused inflation and if government borrowed this diverted funds from productive uses. Thus in almost any shape or form, government intervention in the economy was likely to be harmful. The duty of government was to control money supply and to minimize its other activities.

The new economic approach was, ostensibly at least, taken up by the Thatcher Government with evangelical fervour. As the academic emphasis changed from money supply to market equilibrium and 'supply-side' doctrines this was echoed in economic policy. Thatcher's first Chancellor, Sir Geoffrey Howe, made dramatic efforts to control money supply. Her second, Nigel Lawson, placed his faith in cutting taxes and generating benign 'supply-side' influences. Lawson's Mais Lecture of 1984 argued that governments could not affect the level of employment and that inflation was essentially a monetary phenomenon.[19] In the Chancellor's view, the effects of government attempts to bring down deficit budgets in order to stimulate employment would be foreseen in a private sector where expectations were 'rational', and could only be ineffective and inflationary. The only role for government, therefore, was to liberate the market by reducing distortions and inflexibilities which inhibited 'the enterprise culture'. Thus it appeared that in the half century since the publication of Keynes's *General Theory* the analysis of unemployment had gone from a theory which, in its bowdlerized version, said that only demand was important and that relative prices had no part to play, to one in which supply was accorded the only significant role. We now turn to the links between theory and policy.

Theory and policy

At the end of the 1980s, looking back over the past century it could be said that there had apparently been a remarkably close relationship between economic theory and economic policy. Policy may appear to have followed changes in theory with remarkable rapidity. In fact, a closer examination of the historical relationship suggests that academic theory has traditionally been adapted to circumstances, power structures and to policy pre-requisites.

At the beginning of the interwar period there was a good deal of policy flexibility which came to an abrupt end in 1920 when it became clear that Britain faced a severe deficit on external account and could not, therefore, regain its former international pre-eminence.[20] During the interwar years a very rigid and highly refined version of classical economics was used to justify a situation in which the British price level was seen as being much more important than the level of employment. After 1931 there were some relaxations in these attitudes. Although many academic economists during the interwar years favoured greater provision of public works in order to create employment, this was on political and humanitarian rather than theoretical grounds. It was scarcely surprising that one of the more gifted of them should have sought and found a theoretical justification. However, the ideas of Keynes were ignored by policy-makers until wartime circumstances had removed the unemployment problem.[21]

In the 1940s, despite the influence of the *General Theory*, the creation of the Economic Policy Section of the Treasury and Keynes's apotheosis, it was circumstances rather than theory which dictated policy changes. The white paper on employment policy reflected Keynesian views, but did not indicate that a 'Keynesian revolution' in economic policy had taken place, or was likely to do so. However, in a postwar world of inflationary pressure and tight labour markets, and where a new scale of government intervention was inevitable, a version of Keynesian theory was useful as a rationalization of government macroeconomic management, while free collective bargaining and free enterprise were retained. During the late 1940s and 1950s academics adjusted to the new policy regime and synthesized it with classical economics so that the subject continued to be taught and studied in what was essentially a classical mould. Classical microeconomics remained unchanged and Keynesian notions of macroeconomic adjustment were analysed in classical terms. The concept of general equilibrium was retained and remained central.[22]

In the 1970s new problems of stagflation and recurrent balance of payments crisis produced changes in policy which had remarkably little support from British economists. This continued into the 1980s. In April 1981, 364 academic economists joined in condemning Thatcher's economic policies. A poll of university departments in 1985 found that 80 per cent of economists were in favour of increasing government borrowing in order to boost the economy.[23] However, by the late 1980s most British academic economists were 'neo-Keynesians' who had conceded the main issues and accepted concepts such as the 'natural rate' and 'rational expectations'. They simply objected to the extremes of Thatcherite policy just as their earlier counterparts had favoured public works in the interwar years. By this time the Keynesian case was usually put, if at all, in terms of modest deviations from the classical models, caused, for example by market imperfections or time-lag.[24] The Keynesian view survived but increasingly as a special case in a classical system. Once again, theory had adjusted to historical circumstances and British economists strove to take account of a remarkable chain of events which had confounded their no doubt rational expectations.

Government and administration, finance and business moved to new classical modes of thinking and expression well before such changes began to have a significant impact in the British universities. The origins of policy change owed much to a Conservative tradition which can be traced back to the interwar period and was continued by Thorneycroft and Powell in the postwar years. This was rediscovered at Selsdon and then betrayed by the Heath Government in the early 1970s. Out of the debacle of the Heath Government a small right-wing faction of the party ascended to power at a time when new liberal ideas were emerging in the United States, but again, in response to circumstances. In particular, through Sir Keith Joseph this group had already attempted to embrace new classical concepts and to develop them in a British context. After the downfall of the Heath Government there appeared to be few options or prospects for Conservative government in the face of trade union power. It was clear that such power depended upon full employment but it was assumed that to detract from this was electoral suicide. In these circumstances the new market approach with its emphasis on money supply appeared to provide a rationalization for ending full employment and restoring profitability to British business.[25] It is scarcely surprising, therefore, that Sir Keith Joseph and Margaret Thatcher sought out and embraced what Professor Friedman had to offer. Previous Labour Governments had already been pressed by circumstances into creating what could be seen as precedents and had utilized new economic ideas to justify their actions. With the Conservative victory in 1979 the way was prepared for Britain to join a couple of South American dictatorships in becoming a laboratory for monetarism.[26]

Looking back at the end of the 1980s it appeared that Britain had lurched with enthusiasm from one economic strategy or target to another, as if in search of some Holy Grail of economic policy. William Keegan refers to the 'recurring theme of over-reaction, lack of proportion, and excessive swings of the pendulum of analysis and opinion'.[27] Throughout these years an old economic truth remained: it was not possible to control both the exchange rate and the internal level of economic activity simultaneously. It would be naive to blame the instability to which Keegan refers on economic theory or on particular economic theorists. Over the past century

British economists have struggled, with remarkable persistence and mental ingenuity, to perpetuate and adapt an abstract view of the world to changing political and economic circumstances. In the process the abstract view of how the economy works has scarcely changed at all. The responsibility for policy changes lies with policy-makers and not with economists.

Classical economics, Keynesianism and new classical approaches all rely on market explanations and equilibrium concepts. All failed to explain and predict the real world. In the interwar period the failure of wages to adjust over two decades made classical theory seem inappropriate if not invalid. The Keynesians produced a prescription whereby demand was adjusted, through government intervention, so that it corresponded with supply. This was never tried during the interwar years and would probably not have worked. In the postwar years Keynesian measures were used to make marginal economic adjustments but worked only to a limited and increasingly unsatisfactory extent. Keynesian reflation failed to solve regional and structural problems and strengthened the powerful sections of the labour market at the expense of the weak. The ultimate futility was stagflation – inflation and sharply rising wage costs against a background of heavy unemployment. This represented the worst of all possibilities. The new classical approach also based itself emphatically in market concepts, but in the social laboratory which Britain became in the 1980s, wages continued to rise despite phenomenal increases in unemployment. Again, the market had failed to conform with economic theory.

Since market-based theories have failed in the past and seem likely to fail in the future, and labour economics and related fields have begun to develop useful non-market theories, should the market approach be rejected? Even to ask this question is to commit the ultimate heresy in the eyes of most economists. Faced with the problem of postwar inflation the Keynesian economists advocated wage controls and blamed the trade unions when these failed. When new classical economists gained the ear of government they urged monetary control with the inevitable consequence of unemployment in order to break inflationary expectations. Although price increases were the main problem price control was universally rejected. It was legitimate to control wages or money supply, but direct forms of price control were rejected on the grounds that the market operated through price signals and interference would produce distortions.[28] Market theory is the basis of training in all the main schools of economics and non-market versions emphasizing, for example, environmentalist or Marxist concepts gain little attention although they exist. Of course, markets do exist in the real world and it is certainly possible to identify general tendencies which market theory would predict. However, jumping from this common-sense observation to equilibrium concepts may not be justified. There are also practical questions relating to the efficiency of markets in fulfilling not just economic but also political and social requirements. It is not surprising that previous writers on the subject of unemployment have expressed reservations. According to Guy Routh 'the long established instability of the capitalist economy has now been demonstrated. It is astonishing that the prevailing model presented by university economists should still be one of equilibrium and optimisation, to the neglect of research into the perversities of the real world.'[29] The markets which do exist, whether efficient or not, are all artificial creations representing a particular political, legal, cultural and social reality. The economic system is a social creation and this is what Beveridge had in mind when he asserted:

> Full productive employment in a free society is possible but it is not possible without taking pains. It cannot be won by waving a financial wand; it is a goal that can be reached only by conscious continuous organisation of all our productive resources under democratic control. To win full employment and keep it, we must will the end and must understand and will the means.[30]

VIII

Thatcher's Economic Miracle

'The economic strategy, based on monetarism or neo-classical economics, which was introduced at the end of the 1970s resulted in an increase in unemployment from around one million to around three million. It has now been almost entirely abandoned.' *National Institute of Economic and Social Research, 1987*

'If any would not work, neither should he eat.' *1 Thessalonians 3:10 (quoted by Margaret Thatcher, 1988)*

The Prime Minister of unemployment

Early in 1978 Margaret Thatcher launched an attack in the House of Commons upon the Labour Prime Minister James Callaghan accusing him of creating unemployment. She concluded, 'He will go down in history as the Prime Minister of unemployment.'[1] In the event, it now seems safe to conclude that history will choose to allocate that particular accolade elsewhere.

Thatcherism was made possible by a political fluke in 1975 which brought a relatively minor political figure to the Conservative leadership and enabled a small right-wing faction to 'hijack' the Conservative Party. William Keegan has described how a group of 'evangelicals' eventually forced new economic ideas on the party so that, when they assumed office in 1979, the way was prepared for 'Mrs Thatcher's economic experiment'.[2]

Thatcherism was a blend of old and new ideas skilfully presented by a remarkable political personality, the first female leader of a British political party and someone who was prepared to use the powers of a Prime Minister in new ways. By the 1970s 'new right' political notions were well established in the United States. The

economics of Milton Friedman combined happily with developments in political theory, accounting and what was called 'public
sector decision theory'. All of these relied upon an intellectual
framework which revived nineteenth-century liberal attitudes and
classical economics in particular. Classical notions of a benign
market were applied not only to the economy but also to government and politics. British intellectuals were slow in turning their
attention to these developments; many reacted against them instinc-
tively and most were caught off guard by the simple but powerful
logic involved once neoclassical axioms were accepted.

But not all was new. It has been emphasized that the ideas
themselves had eighteenth- and nineteenth-century antecedents, but
also there were important real world precedents. The modern
Conservative Party, pre-Thatcher, was pragmatic and paternalistic
and it was often alleged that Thatcherism was at odds with this
tradition and a throwback to nineteenth-century liberalism. There
was much truth in these claims, but it must also be pointed out that
Thatcherism was the apotheosis of a minority but well-recognized
postwar conservative view most often associated with Peter
Thorneycroft and Enoch Powell.[3] This view is also evident in the
'Selsdon' programme which preceded and guided the Heath
Government of 1970–4. Most commentators have overlooked the
remarkable parallels between Thatcherism and what might be
termed the Chamberlainism of the 1930s. Although very different in
personality and style, both Margaret Thatcher and Neville
Chamberlain combined authoritarianism and a belief in the power
of law to force change with free market philosophy. Chamberlain
claimed that governments had no more chance of controlling
unemployment than they had of influencing the weather. In the
1980s similar views were being put forward by Nigel Lawson on
behalf of the Thatcher Government.

In the postwar period the 'sound money' Conservatives were
largely submerged by the success of 'Butskellism' until the 1970s.
With the problems of that decade a re-emergence was not unlikely
and, inadvertently, the ground was prepared by Labour Governments which undermined belief in collective action, cut areas of

public spending, established targets for money supply, and abandoned the traditional approach to full employment in the face of
economic crisis. By 1979 circumstances and new ideas were moving
in the same direction. A new climate of opinion regarding the state
and state activity was emerging. In part, this reflected growing
disenchantment towards state welfare from burgeoning higher
income earners who resented progressive taxation as social benefits
became increasingly selective or devalued. Inflation and 'fiscal creep'
caused increasing numbers to feel that the tax burden was excessive.
The new economics had gained a major influence in private sector
finance and new attitudes were also beginning to make an impact in
the upper levels of the Civil Service. By the late 1970s it was possible
to predict, on a world-wide basis, a gradual diminution of government activities and influence. In Britain in 1979 this development
was given the impact of an unusual political personality. Once in
power Thatcher pursued her objectives ruthlessly and in evangelical
terms. This involved the gradual elimination of opposition in the
Cabinet, the Civil Service and throughout public corporations and
other bodies owned or controlled by the state. There was also a
willingness to undertake confrontation where necessary, but this
was usually done with careful preparation and foresight.

When they assumed office in 1979 the leading members of the
Thatcher Government must have assumed that the policies which
they intended to pursue would probably lead to a sharp increase in
unemployment. In his Preston speech of 1974 Sir Keith Joseph,
widely regarded as Thatcher's mentor, had come dangerously close
for a politician to openly advocating unemployment as a panacea for
Britain's economic ills.[4] During the 1970s Friedman and other
economists spoke in terms of a 'short, sharp shock' of unemployment as a means of breaking inflationary expectations in the
economy. What was not anticipated was that unemployment would
rise so rapidly as it did, or that it would remain so high for so long.
The restrictive fiscal stance and crude monetarist experiment
introduced by the Thatcher Government coincided with and intensified recession which was aggravated by the second oil shock. The
result for the British economy was very damaging. Although most

industrial economies were adversely affected by the rise in oil prices associated with the commencement of the Iran–Iraq war, and restrictive economic policies, for combined reasons of dogma and crisis, were widely applied, Britain was unmatched in loss of jobs and product.

Even though the Government massively overran its target for growth in money supply, the effort to reach targets had far reaching and highly damaging effects on the economy and adverse social consequences. High interest rates pushed the exchange rate, already bolstered by the onflow of North Sea oil, to levels which destroyed large sections of British industry. Export industries lost markets but even more destruction resulted from import penetration. Meanwhile, fiscal policy involved increases in taxation combined with severe cuts in spending. Allowing for unemployment, this represented a very sharp degree of fiscal tightening. The inevitable result was a very sharp increase in unemployment and severe damage to the economy. The contraction forced many companies into liquidation. In these circumstances it is clear why manufacturing industry had to bear the brunt of adversity and why the major part of unemployment was generated in this sector. Most of the service sector did not export or compete with imports. Of course, it was possible to lay the blame elsewhere and, as usual, on the trade unions. The Medium Term Financial Strategy had set out rolling four-year moving targets for growth in money supply and workers and unions had failed to modify wage demands accordingly. However, such an approach was, to say the least, naive. The failure to come near targets for M3 (defined as notes plus bank deposits) was inevitable since the nature of money was changing for a variety of reasons including deregulation, new financial techniques, and easier bank credit induced in part by the profits which accrued to financial institutions as a result of high interest rates. While the Public Sector Borrowing requirement could be controlled bank credit could not. In effect, the Government raised interest rates to very high levels in real terms in order to control an erratic measure of money supply. This, in turn, precipitated a rise in sterling which was further boosted by the second oil shock and the onflow of

North Sea oil. Damaging consequences in terms of exports, import penetration and unemployment were inevitable. The severe down-turn was compounded by the 1981 budget which did much to ensure a slow upturn. By 1982 the monetarist experiment was over but the withdrawal had to be dignified and financial opinion still demanded to be placated by monetarist jargon. New targets were enunciated (M1 and PSL2 and later M0) but the search for a talisman eventually settled on the exchange rate after the 1987 election. In the Government's first three years 20 per cent of British industry had been wiped out, GDP had fallen by 5 per cent, in spite of North Sea oil, and unemployment had trebled to levels not considered possible during the postwar period and at least as bad as during the depression of the 1930s.

Although the Thatcher Government had repeatedly made the assertion that unemployment was international and part of a problem which afflicted all industrial economies, this was simply not true. In 1984, for example, when the officially recorded level of unemployment in the UK was 13.2 per cent, there were European countries with higher levels, including Belgium (14.0), the Nether-lands (14.0) and Spain (20.2). However, several industrial econo-mies had much lower levels, for example: Switzerland (1.2), Sweden (3.1), Norway (3.0), Japan (2.7) and Austria (3.8).[5] These unemployment differentials between major industrial economies have continued throughout the 1980s and this suggests, quite clearly, that domestic conditions and policies may be more impor-tant than international circumstances in promoting or preventing unemployment.

In a work entitled *Why Some Peoples Are More Unemployed than Others*, Goran Therborn studied the causes of unemployment in sixteen industrial economies and concluded:[6] 'The existence or non-existence of an institutionalised commitment to full employment is the basic explanation for the differential impact of the current crisis.' Thus the explanation is essentially political and policy-based. Therborn also concludes that the shortest and fastest route to mass unemployment was to be found in the 'cut the public sector, strengthen the market economy' approach of the Thatcher Government.[7]

After the debacle

Politically the Thatcher regime was extremely fortunate in surviving the dramatic increase in unemployment and the economic decline which occurred during its first term. In part it was possible to blame adversity on international forces and to point to increases in unemployment elsewhere. However, there appeared to be a direct correlation between unemployment and restrictive economic policies and Britain was in a relatively extreme position in terms of adversity. The Government survived through a combination of political skill and good fortune. There were three particular pieces of good luck: firstly, the onflow of North Sea oil, which, apart from its general impact on income and wealth, improved government revenues and temporarily solved the long-standing balance of payments problem. Britain, and the Thatcher Government, were extremely fortunate in that the peak of North Sea oil production more or less coincided with the peaking of international oil prices. It has frequently been pointed out that the Government made no effort to ensure that some of the proceeds of this heaven-sent bonanza were used to promote long-run benefit for the British economy and that the bounty of North Sea oil was 'wasted through unemployment'.[8] Secondly, it was fortunate for the Government that the 1983 General Election appears to have been dominated by the British recapture of the Falkland Islands and the electorate suspended judgement on the management of the economy. Thirdly, the Opposition was weakened by divisions and ineffective leadership. In the early 1980s a group of right-wing Labour politicians became disaffected and eventually formed the Social Democratic Party which worked with the Liberals. From this time government with a minority of votes became possible and a three-party system similar to that which prevailed in the interwar years was established.

With this political and economic good fortune and her undoubted political skills Thatcher was able to survive what was perhaps the most unfortunate episode in modern British economic policy. In the

1920s and the early 1970s Britain would have faced severe problems regardless of policy. In the early 1980s a wisely managed British economy, with the bounty of North Sea oil, might have stolen a march on the world and dramatically reversed relative decline. Instead, Britain was pushed into absolute decline and mass unemployment. However, the burdens of policy disaster were unevenly shared with the brunt falling upon the public sector and the poorer sections and regions. Although labelled 'the Iron Lady' Thatcher showed remarkable indecision and vacillation as her administration lurched from one policy to another. After a succession of monetary targets had proved to be beyond control there was a gradual retreat from the monetarist dogma while comparisons with the Heath administration and talk of 'U-turns' were hotly denied. Having stumbled into mass unemployment and managed to escape political retribution, the regime made a virtue of necessity and refused to attack the problem in traditional ways as the Heath Government had done in 1972. Without unemployment Thatcherism would undoubtedly have failed.

It was unemployment which broke the national power of the trade union movement and intimidated sections of the working class so that traditional solidarity collapsed. Fears of job loss at all levels, and especially in the public sector, intimidated workers into submission to new policies. Above all, unemployment was crucial to the longer run 'restructuring' of the economy which both government and business demanded. Those firms which survived the debacle of the early 1980s were able to benefit from improved productivity and a very different kind of labour supply situation in which managerial prerogatives could be reasserted through fear in the workplace.

In the most famous confrontation with the miners in 1985 the basic question at issue was employment and the power struggle was decided, in large part, by the effects of unemployment.[9] The NUM came close to success despite the Government's willingness to use all the resources of the state, regardless of cost. They failed because other labour organizations and workers failed to give the kind of support which was expected and the miners themselves were divided. There were issues between different leaders but, at a deeper level, there was an absence of spontaneous industrial support for the miners. Lorry drivers were willing to co-operate with working miners in breaking the strike and railway workers already felt that their jobs were at risk. These fears, generated by economic insecurity, were basic to the outcome, although the media trivialized the event into personality issues. In the General Strike of 1926 the miners' leaders made serious tactical errors and also suffered from highly adverse press comment and vilification, and there were accusations of TUC and Labour Party betrayal. However, in 1926 the trade union movement demonstrated its potential strength.[10] In 1985–6 it revealed its weakness in the face of unemployment.

The disaster of the early 1980s and the precipitation of mass unemployment in Britain is comparable with the sharp downturn of 1920–1. On both occasions there were policy mistakes based on false assumptions and political predispositions. These combined with adverse international circumstances and had devastating effects on Britain's peculiar economic vulnerabilities. The result on each occasion was a spectacular rise in unemployment which could not be fully reversed for many years, even with improved rates of economic growth. On the positive side there were gains in productivity which appear to have been sustained. In part, labour 'shake-out' and management aggression may have made some contribution to productivity gains, although clear evidence for this is lacking. In the interwar years it is clear that Britain's fundamental economic weakness remained and continued to the Second World War. Unemployment remained as a social disaster which seared itself into the national conscience. Unemployment gave no stimulus to new industries and the exaggerated decline in traditional industrial areas intensified the weakness on external account. In the long run it may also be concluded that much of the suffering and loss of the 1980s was unnecessary and could have been avoided; also that the benefits which accrued were slight and might have been achieved in less painful and more effective ways. Since the interwar period full employment has remained as one of the most important goals of a successful economic policy.

The achievement

Of course, it is much too soon to attempt a considered historical assessment of the Thatcher years. By the late 1980s it was clear that there had been substantial real income improvements and that, for a short time, Britain had grown faster than other European economies. In some quarters it was being claimed that the Government had performed an economic miracle. These views ignored unemployment which remained much higher than in any other postwar decade. Even on the much-criticized and misleading official figures it remained at about 7 per cent at the late 1980s peak. Unemployment was no longer seen as a tragedy facing the nation; it had been talked down and marginalized into a non-problem.

Similar attitudes might well have prevailed at the end of the 1930s if Neville Chamberlain had possessed national income statistics and greater presentational skills. As Peden has pointed out, 'economic policy after 1931 was a remarkable mixture of orthodoxy and innovation'.[11] By 1939 Britain had experienced eight years of growth and most of them at higher rates than in the 1980s; unemployment on the official figures, which had not been tampered with, had fallen from 23 per cent in 1931 to around 10 per cent in 1938; there had been remarkable growth in productivity and industrial output; Britain had made up lost ground against the United States and other major industrial nations; real incomes had probably risen faster than in any decade since the Black Death; industrial output, real wages and consumer spending had broken new records; house prices had fallen and new homes had been built and acquired at an unprecedented rate; and there had been a major improvement in the balance of payments.[12] These facts may not fit the conventional image of the 1930s and they serve to illustrate how selected facts, or statistics, can make or break impressions; also that measuring from the trough of a depression to the following peak may create the illusion of progress.

There are more ways than one to run an economy and there are always alternatives. The governments of the 1930s are perceived in dismal terms not because they failed to deliver economic growth but because they failed to eradicate mass unemployment and failed to prevent the growth of 'fascism'. Economic growth is endemic to modern industrial society and the aim of economic policy is to create acceptable circumstances for growth and to arrange for growth to be sustained. Growth is normal and the British economy in the postwar period has grown more rapidly than ever before. Achieving growth as such has not been the problem; the real difficulty has been in reconciling growth with price and exchange rate stability. This problem re-emerged in 1988 and there were serious doubts that fundamental economic weaknesses had been eradicated despite a decade of economic 'experiment' and mass unemployment. It remains to be seen if history will view the 1980s and Margaret Thatcher in a better light than the 1930s and Neville Chamberlain. Chamberlain's dictator proved more durable than General Galtieri. On the other hand, Chamberlain as Chancellor and Prime Minister did not preside over the precipitation of mass unemployment, merely its continuation. Interwar governments may not have done much to tackle unemployment but they did not attempt to minimize it. Indeed it has been suggested that, by the end of the interwar period, unemployment was the reference point against which all government policies had to be tested. [13]

Ideas and reality

Under Thatcherism the principles of market economics were followed in a pragmatic way and free enterprise evangelism was reserved for special occasions. Where market principles failed to conform with and to enhance right-wing Conservative aims they were abandoned and inevitably this gave rise to accusations of hypocrisy which were encouraged by Thatcher's tendency to preach and even, on at least one occasion, take to the pulpit. Thus it was acceptable to introduce legislation which curbed and weakened trade unions, but few new measures were introduced to improve corporate control or to limit widespread business monopolies and restrictive practices. State expenditure had to be reduced, but in some areas – defence, law and order, the Falklands, Northern Ireland – it was possible to make massive outlays regardless of cost. Similarly, vast public expense was sanctioned in order to 'see off' the miners and enormous debts were written off at the taxpayers' expense in order to make publicly-owned industries attractive for 'sale to the public' or 'privatization'. De-regulation in all its forms was highly selective. The double standard also extended to subsidization which, for example, was legitimate for English agriculture but not for coal-mining.

Undoubtedly some gains were made through the elimination of restrictive practices by labour, although the reduced costs which resulted from technical change in Fleet Street newspapers, for example, were not reflected in prices charged to consumers. While attacks were made on professional groups in the public sector, private sector professions retained their privileges. Threats to solicitors and opticians left the market for their services basically unchanged. Fiscal changes were uneven and highly inequitable and this gave added credence to the accusation that the 'market principles' of Thatcherism were far from being theoretically pure. Adam Smith, one assumes, would have been highly critical of a system stacked in favour of producers and against consumers. Although consumer protection was treated with an indifference verging on contempt, the Labour Party failed to expose this or to take the clear opportunity of championing consumers. One of the basic aims of Thatcherism was to enhance profitability in British business and this was achieved at considerable social cost. Social justice, worker protection, full employment, consumer and environmental interests were largely ignored in the process and, ironically, the Opposition, instead of springing to the defence of the electoral majority, resorted to a process of imitation under the heading of 'market socialism'.

By the late 1980s the Government began to exhibit some belated awareness of these criticisms. Thatcher began to give some rhetorical attention to 'green' or environmental issues and proposals to 'reform' the legal and medical professions were produced against a chorus of practitioner opposition.

Did Thatcherism amount to anything more than a charter for greed? A crude attempt to bolster profits which could be analysed in simple and classic Marxist terms? If this was the case then it can only be said that both the rhetoric and the rationale were brilliant and very effectively presented. It is possible for leaders as well as followers to believe their own propaganda. The British business-men who in a monopolistic world exuded free market philosophy came from a long tradition of hypocrisy. During the late nineteenth century the inequities and exploitation of Victorian society had been cloaked in an avalanche of lower middle-class homilies which were revived and gave rise to frequent references to 'Victorian values' and the Thatcher corner shop in Grantham. It was true that Thatcher was a grocer's daughter, but what was often overlooked was the fact that she was a millionaire's wife, leading a cabinet of millionaires, and pursuing policies which did much more for millionaires than small shopkeepers.

By the late 1980s the extent of Thatcher's economic achievements were being called into question. The fundamental British economic problems with wages, investment and the balance of payments clearly remained unsolved. Throughout the 1980s wages rose much more rapidly than prices and this tended to undermine dogmatic views about the influence of trade unions and the effects of unemployment on wages. While some wage adjustment did occur, it was not as widespread as might have been expected. Regional and other differentials may have widened, but not as anticipated. The wage experience of the 1980s tended to make nonsense of some of the most firmly held theories of the 1970s. As in the interwar period, it appeared that wages had failed to adjust and there had been sustained improvements in real wages in the face of mass unemploy-ment. It has been suggested that the ultimate guarantee of the interwar wage structure was the introduction of a more or less universal system of unemployment benefits from the early 1920s.[14] Non-labour costs fell and productivity rose, so both wages and profits were able to improve. Union bargaining power was weak-ened and membership fell sharply, but trade unions were not destroyed and bargaining potential remained. In the 1980s, as in the 1930s, the shift in the terms of trade and rising productivity made significant real wage improvements possible at the same time as rising profits. Both were crucial to the success of Thatcherism.

Like interwar administrations the Thatcher Government

demanded pay restraint and wage concessions which in general did not materialize. Indeed, there was something hypocritical about a government which openly sanctioned greed in the name of wealth creation but demanded that wage-earners should exercise restraint. Incomes restraint was much more successful in the public sector than in the private where it proved easier to attack jobs than wages. In 1987 it seemed probable that real wage improvements in the private sector were a crucial factor in creating the essential electoral minority which sustained the Government in a third General Election victory. Although welfare benefits were eroded in real and relative terms, and increasingly subject to more stringent regulations, there was no attempt to abolish or radically reform the system. [15] Even for a 'tough' regime the total withdrawal of support was politically unthinkable. 'Workfare'-type solutions were rejected on grounds of expense and complexity, except on a limited basis as in the YTS. [16] This was generally avoided by middle-class youth and widely regarded as a 'cheap labour' subsidy to employers. By the late 1980s the Government was under some pressure from its own supporters to extend this kind of solution to the long-term unemployed and beyond. Increasingly, therefore, there was emphasis on search, training and work in return for unemployment benefits which became more stringent and were eroded in real terms. In general it may be said that wages were not traded for employment, if that were possible, and there are direct parallels with the 1930s.

Although the Thatcher Government did much to assist the employer the response from manufacturing industry was disappointing. In part this reflected the economic devastation of the early 1980s when so much capacity was destroyed. Productivity improved, but output was slow in regaining the peak levels of the previous decade and industrial investment failed to recover. Between 1980 and 1986 the demand for manufactured goods rose by 15 per cent while output only rose 4 per cent. It is scarcely surprising that imports rose 40 per cent and Britain became a net importer of manufactured goods for the first time in recorded history. Even before the Industrial Revolution Britain had been a net exporter of manufactures. A £5.5 billion export surplus in 1980 was turned into an £20.0 billion deficit by 1989. Although there was some compensation from oil and services it was clear from the mid-1980s that the balance of payments was deteriorating and use of the exchange rate to curb inflation pointed the way towards a 'good old-fashioned sterling crisis'.[17]

In a review of British economic growth before and since 1979 Professor Nick Crafts has joined others in questioning the Thatcher economic miracle. Growth rates of real output per worker employed during 1979–87 were better than during the crisis years of the 1970s, but not as good as during the 1950s and 1960s.[18] Significant productivity improvements were recorded in manufacturing but these were paid for in terms of increased work intensity and stress in employment, a general disregard for workers' rights and safety at work, 'fear in the workplace' for those in jobs and, above all, through the perpetration of mass unemployment. It was not clear that the productivity improvements which had taken place could be sustained.

By the middle of 1989 Britain faced a record balance of payments deficit, a problem with lack of confidence in sterling and the worst inflation of any major industrial economy. While many commentators blamed these problems on the Chancellor's tax cuts in the previous year, excessive credit creation and poor short-term macroeconomic management, the real problems were much more fundamental. The original experiment with monetarism had been a disastrous failure and the 'supply-side revolution' which had succeeded it had been extremely partial and of limited value. Some limited gains had been made, in terms of higher productivity and profits, but the governmental contribution, rhetoric aside, had been delivered through attacks on wage-earners by trade union 'reform' and through mass unemployment. As unemployment fell it became increasingly clear that labour market legislation alone could not achieve pay restraint or sound industrial relations. The main instrument of the economic 'miracle' had been unemployment. Now it appeared that 2 million unemployed, on the official figures, was insufficient!

During the 1980s the Thatcher Government repeatedly made claims that it was solving Britain's supply-side problems but its only major contribution to this lay in the creation, through a mixture of accident and design, of mass unemployment. A genuine supply-side improvement required measures to promote the increased supply and improved quality of labour and capital. In particular, improvements in education, both in vocational and general terms, improvements in training for managers and workers, improved research and development, higher investment in the domestic economy and genuine improvements in industrial relations. Britain's record in these areas remained poor in terms of international comparison. Throughout the 1980s scientific and medical researchers were harassed by cost-cutting and reorganization. A university system which had been envied throughout the world was urged to adopt the methods, aims and organization of British industry which was renowned for its poor productivity performance and bad industrial relations. An increasing number of potential students were denied university places and schools were subjected to severe resource limitations. By 1988 the combination of 'macho' economic management and public sector neglect threatened not only the quality of life but also the continuation of economic growth. Although unemployment remained, on the official figures at around 2 million, severe labour and skill shortages were becoming apparent. Thus the economy was getting the worst of all possible worlds and there were few signs that Britain's long-standing problem of low productivity and lack of competitiveness had been solved. Through the divisive years of the 1980s the majority of the British electorate had continued to vote against Thatcherism but circumstances contrived to give the Government the benefit of the doubt, not least because some were persuaded that material success was being delivered. Once this was called into question the 1980s were on their way to acquiring some of the bleak connotations of the 1930s. The hope remained that during the 1990s there *would* be an alternative.

Notes

I Introduction

1 D. N. Ashton, *Unemployment under Capitalism* (Brighton, 1988), pp. 82–114.

2 D. H. Aldcroft, *Full Employment: The Elusive Goal* (Brighton, 1984), pp. 157–61.

3 B. Jones, *Sleepers Wake! Technology and the Future of Work* (Brighton, 1982); J. I. Gershuny and I. D. Miles, *The New Service Economy* (1982).

4 C. Jenkins and B. Sherman, *The Collapse of Work* (1979); B. Showler and A. Sinfield (eds.), *The Workless State* (Oxford, 1981); B. Jordon, *Mass Unemployment and the Future of Britain* (Oxford, 1982).

5 J. E. King (ed.), *Readings in Labour Economics* (Oxford, 1980).

6 M. J. Daunton, *A Property-Owning Democracy? Housing in Britain* (1987), pp. 117–19.

7 Goran Therborn, *Why Some Peoples Are More Unemployed than Others: The Strange Paradox of Growth and Employment* (1986), pp. 91–101.

8 Gavyn Davies, *Governments Can Affect Employment: A Critique of Monetarism – Old and New* (1986); Peter Sinclair, *Unemployment: Economic Theory and Evidence* (Oxford, 1987), ch. 16.

9 S. Glynn and A. E. Booth (eds.), *The Road to Full Employment* (1987), Introduction.

10 D. Marsden, *The End of Economic Man? Custom and Competition in Labour Markets* (Brighton, 1986).

11 R. E. Pahl, *Divisions of Labour* (Oxford, 1984).

12 K. Kumar, 'Unemployment as a Problem in the Development of Industrial Societies: The English Experience', *Sociological Review*, 32, no. 2 (May 1984) pp. 185–233.

13 E. F. Schumacher, *Good Work* (1979), p. 2.

14 R. Smith, *Unemployment and Health: A Disaster and a Challenge* (Oxford, 1987), ch. 5.

15 R. M. Solow, 'On Theories of Unemployment', Presidential Address 92nd Meeting of American Economics Association (Atlanta, 1979), p. 8.

16 R. M. Blackburn and M. Mann, *The Working Class in the Labour Market* (1979).

17 R. E. Pahl, 'Employment, Work and the Domestic Division of Labour', *International Journal of Urban and Regional Research*, 4 (1980), pp. 1–20.

18 J. H. Treble, *Urban Poverty in Britain* (1979).

19 J. J. Hughes and R. Perlman, *The Economics of Unemployment: A Comparative Analysis of Britain and the United States* (Brighton, 1984), pp. 34–6.

20 N. Crafts, *Brtish Economic Growth before and after 1979: A Review of the Evidence* (Centre for Economic Policy Research, Discussion Paper No. 292, 1989), pp. 30–1; E. Batstone, 'Labour and Productivity', *Oxford Review of Economic Policy*, 2 (1987), pp. 32–43.

21 A. E. Booth, 'Corporatism, Capitalism and Depression in Twentieth Century Britain', *British Journal of Sociology*, 33 (1982), pp. 210–12.

22 Glynn and Booth, pp. 43–56.

23 Hugo Young, *One of Us* (1989).

24 Crafts, pp. 32–4.

25 N. Lawson, 'Thatcherism in Practice: A Progress Report', *Address to the Zurich Society of Economics*, 14 January 1981, HM Treasury.

II Measuring Unemployment

1 C. Johnson, *Measuring the Economy* (1988), p. 82.

2 W. R. Garside, *The Measurement of Unemployment: Methods and Sources in Great Britain, 1850–1979* (Oxford, 1980).

3 J. Harris, *William Beveridge: A Biography* (Oxford, 1977), p. 83.

4 G. D. N. Worswick (ed.), *The Concept and Measurement of Involuntary Unemployment* (1976).

5 J. J. Hughes, 'The Measurement of Unemployment: An Exercise in Political Economy', *Industrial Relations*, VII (1976–7), pp. 4–12.

6 C. H. Feinstein, *National Income, Expenditure and Output of the United Kingdom, 1855–1965* (Cambridge, 1972), p. 225.

7 N. K. Buxton and D. I. Mackay, *British Employment Statistics: A Guide to Sources and Methods* (Oxford, 1976), ch. 1.

8 G. Stedman Jones, *Outcast London* (Oxford, 1971), pp. 19–158.

9 J. H. Treble, *Urban Poverty in Britain* (1979), p. 13.

10 Treble, p. 53.

11 Treble, ch. 2.

12 DoE, *British Labour Statistics: Historical Abstract, 1886–1968* (1971).

13 DoE, *British Labour Statistics*.

14 C. Clark, *National Income and Outlay* (1937), pp. 31–2.
15 John Hilton, 'Statistics of the Unemployed Derived from the Workings of the Unemployment Acts', *Journal of the Royal Statistical Society*, XLVI (1923), pp. 154–93.
16 Barry Eichengreen, 'Unemployment in Interwar Britain: Dole or Doldrums?', *Oxford Economic Papers*, 39, pp. 597–623.
17 S. Glynn and A. Booth, *British Unemployment in the Interwar Period: Survey and Perspective* (Canberra, 1983), pp. 6–7.
18 Feinstein, p. 221 and Table 56, T123.
19 A. Chapman and R. Knight, *Wages and Salaries in the United Kingdom, 1920–1938* (Cambridge, 1953).
20 See below.
21 Garside, p. 49; Glynn and Booth, p.7.
22 D. Metcalf, S. J. Nickell and N. Floros, 'Still Searching for an Explanation of Unemployment in Inter-War Britain', *Journal of Political Economy*, 90 (1982), p. 210.
23 *Department of Employment Gazette* (monthly).
24 J. Wood, *How Much Unemployment* (IEA, 1972); J. Bourlet and A. Bell, *Unemployment and Inflation: The Need for a Trustworthy Unemployment Indicator* (Economic Research Council, 1973).
25 *The Times*, 6 September 1972.
26 J. J. Hughes, 'How Should We Measure Unemployment?', *British Journal of Industrial Relations*, XII, 3 (1975); M. Peston, 'Unemployment: Why We Need a New Measurement', *Lloyds Bank Review*, April 1972.
27 J. Wood, *How Little Unemployment* (IEA, 1975) and 'The Unemployment Statistics and Their Interpretation', *Department of Employment Gazette*, March 1975.
28 A. R. Thatcher in Worswick (1976).
29 K. Hawkins, *Unemployment* (1984), pp. 15–16.
30 According to the Unemployment Unit the method of counting unemployment had been revised twenty-five times under the Thatcher Government to March 1989. Three further changes were projected.
31 *Observer*, 17 August 1986.
32 *Observer*, 14 May 1989.
33 The Labour Force Survey was carried out biennially during 1973–83 and annually thereafter. It was based on interviews of a representative random sample of 60,000 households.
34 Quoted in *Guardian*, 9 March 1987.
35 A. Deacon, *In Search of the Scrounger* (1976).
36 A. Booth and S. Glynn, 'Unemployment in the Interwar Period: A

Multiple Problem', *Journal of Contemporary History*, 10 (1975), pp. 614–15.

37 Stedman Jones, *Outcast London*.

38 C. H. Lee, *British Regional Employment Statistics, 1841–1971* (Cambridge, 1979).

39 Barry Eichengreen, 'Unemployment in Interwar Britain', *Refresh*, 8 (Spring 1989), p. 3.

40 *DoE Gazette*.

41 R. Layard, *How to Beat Unemployment* (Oxford, 1986), ch. 8; K. Walsh, *Long-term Unemployment: An International Perspective* (1986).

42 M. Jahoda, P. Lazarsfeld and Hans Zeisal, *Die Arbeitslosen von Marienthal* (Vienna, 1933).

43 P. Eisenberg and P. Lazarsfeld, 'The Psychological Effects of Unemployment', *Psychological Bulletin*, 35, 6 (June 1938), p. 378.

44 L. Beales and R. S. Lambert (eds.), *Memoirs of the Unemployed* (1934); for a modern example of this approach to unemployment see D. Marsden, *Workless: An Exploration of the Social Context between the Worker and Society* (Brighton, 1982).

45 Layard, ch. 8.

46 N. F. R. Crafts, 'Long-term Unemployment in Britain in the 1930s', *Economic History Review*, XL, 3 (August 1987), Table 1, p. 420.

47 Walsh, p. 99.

48 There is an extensive literature on youth unemployment in the 1970s and 1980s. See, for example: M. White (ed.), *The Social World of the Young Unemployed* (PSI, 1987); S. Walker and L. Barton, *Youth, Unemployment and Schooling* (Milton Keynes, 1986).

49 Glynn and Booth, p. 9.

50 B. Eichengreen, 'Juvenile Unemployment in 20th Century Britain: The Emergence of a Problem', *Social Research*, 54 (1987), pp. 273–302.

51 Walker and Barton, p. 2.

52 C. Wallace, *For Richer, for Poorer, Growing up in and out of Work* (1987).

53 P. Southgate, 'The Disturbances of July, 1981 in Handsworth', *Public Disorder*, 72 (1982).

54 S. Box and C. Hale, 'Economic Crisis and the Rising Prison Population in England and Wales', *Crime and Social Justice*, 17 (Summer 1982).

55 D. M. Shephard and B. M. Barraclough, 'Work and Suicide: An Empirical Investigation', *British Journal of Psychiatry*, 136 (May 1980).

56 White, p. 1.

57 Economist Intelligence Unit, *Coping with Unemployment: The Effects on the Unemployed Themselves* (1982).

58 C. Clark, *National Income and Outlay* (1937), p. 30.

59 C. Bean, R. Layard and S. Nickell, *The Rise in Unemployment* (Oxford, 1986), p. 123.
60 S. Fineman, *White Collar Unemployment: Impact and Stress* (1983).
61 Eichengreen, *Refresh*, p. 3.

III Understanding Unemployment

1 T. W. Hutchison, *A Review of Economic Doctrines* (Oxford, 1953), p. 409.
2 J. Harris, *Unemployment and Politics* (Oxford, 1972), pp. 11–15.
3 G. Stedman Jones, *Outcast London* (Oxford, 1971), Part I, pp. 19–158; J. H. Treble, *Urban Poverty in Britain* (1979).
4 J. J. Hughes and R. Perlman, *The Economics of Unemployment: A Comparative Analysis of Britain and the United States* (Brighton, 1984), p. 27.
5 D. H. Aldcroft, *Full Employment: The Elusive Goal* (Brighton, 1984), pp. 1–20.
6 J. K. Galbraith, *The Great Crash* (New York, 1946); M. Friedman and A. Schwartz, *Monetary Trends in the United States and the United Kingdom* (Chicago, 1982).
7 In the real world even those markets which may be said to approach perfection usually require a substantial legal and institutional framework.
8 Hutchison, p. 420.
9 K. Marx, *Capital*, I (1867, 1954 edn), p. 593.
10 Hutchison, p. 410.
11 Hutchison, p. 412.
12 Hutchison, p. 119.
13 Hutchison, p. 348.
14 D. Marsden, *The End of Economic Man? Custom and Competition in Labour Markets* (Brighton, 1986), p. 184.
15 W. R. Garside, 'The Real Wage Debate and British Interwar Unemployment' in S. Glynn and A. E. Booth (eds.), *The Road to Full Employment* (1987).
16 S. Glynn and J. Oxborrow, *Interwar Britain* (1976), pp. 248–60.
17 S. Glynn, 'Real Policy Options', in Glynn and Booth (1987).
18 M. Friedman, 'The Role of Monetary Policy', *American Economic Review*, 58 (March 1968).
19 D. K. Benjamin and L. A. Kochin, 'Searching for an Explanation of Unemployment in Inter-War Britain', *Journal of Political Economy*, 87 (1979).

20 For various replies to Kochin and Benjamin see the *Journal of Political Economy*, 90 (1982).

21 M. Bruno and J. D. Sachs, *The Economics of Worldwide Stagflation* (1985).

22 P. Minford, *Unemployment: Cause and Cure* (Oxford, 1983).

23 D. Marsden, *The End of Economic Man?* (Brighton, 1986).

24 F. Wilkinson (ed.), *The Dynamics of Labour Market Segmentation* (1981); R. Loveridge and A. L. Mok, *Theories of Labour Market Segmentation* (The Hague, 1979).

25 E. Friedson, 'Occupational Autonomy and Labour Market Shelters', in P. L. Stewart and M. G. Cantor, *Varieties of Work* (1982).

26 For useful surveys see Marsden (1986) and D. N. Ashton, *Unemployment under Capitalism: The Sociology of British and American Labour Markets* (Brighton, 1986).

27 A. Oswald, 'The Microeconomic Theory of the Trade Union', *Economic Journal*, 92, 367 (1983).

28 P. Doeringer and M. J. Piore, *Internal Labour Markets and Manpower Analysis* (Levington, 1971).

29 Marsden, ch. 2.

30 R. M. Solow, *On Theories of Unemployment* (Atlanta, 1979), p. 3.

31 R. Layard, *How to Beat Unemployment* (Oxford, 1986), ch. 5.

32 R. Clarke, *Work in Crisis: The Dilemma of a Nation* (Edinburgh, 1982), p. xv.

IV The Emergence of Unemployment

1 J. A. Garraty, *Unemployment in History* (New York, 1978).

2 C. Cipolla, *Before the Industrial Revolution: European Society and Economy, 1600–1750* (1976), p. 13.

3 Quoted by Cipolla, p. 13.

4 J. de Vries, *Economy of Europe in an Age of Crisis, 1600–1750* (Cambridge, 1976), p. 83.

5 N. F. R. Crafts, *British Economic Growth during the Industrial Revolution* (1985), pp. 38–44.

6 J. Northcott and P. Rogers, *Microelectronics in Industry: What's Happening in Britain* (PSI, 1982).

7 C. Leadbeater and J. Lloyd, *In Search of Work* (1987), pp. 82–100; S. Williams, *A Job to Live: The Impact of Tomorrow's Technology on Work and Society* (1985), pp. 53–9; J. I. Gershuny and I. D. Miles, *The New Service Economy* (1983).

8 D. Bythel, *The Handloom Weavers* (Cambridge, 1969).

9 M. Olson, 'The Political Economy of Comparative Growth Rates', in

D. C. Mueller (ed.), *The Political Economy of Growth* (New Haven, 1983).

10 G. Stedman Jones, *Outcast London* (Oxford, 1971).

11 E. J. Hobsbawm, *Industry and Empire* (1969), p. 85.

12 J. Lewis, *Women in England, 1870–1950* (Brighton, 1984), pp. 145–205.

13 R. C. O. Matthews, C. H. Feinstein and J. C. Odling-Smee, *British Economic Growth, 1856–1973* (Oxford, 1982), pp. 82–3.

14 K. Marx, *Capital* (Moscow, 1961), pp. 631–2.

15 P. H. Lindert and J. C. Williamson, 'English Workers' Living Standards during the Industrial Revolution. A New Look', *Economic History Review*, XXXVI (1983).

16 J. Harris, *Unemployment and Politics* (Oxford, 1972), p. 1. For a different view see J. H. Treble, *Urban Poverty in Britain* (1979), p. 51.

17 S. B. Saul, *The Myth of the Great Depression, 1873–1896* (1973).

18 D. Winch, *Economics and Policy: A Historical Study* (1969), part 1.

19 Harris, *Unemployment and Politics*, pp. 4 and 7.

20 A. C. Pigou, *Unemployment* (1913).

21 *16th Annual Report of the Local Government Board*, quoted by Harris, p. 43.

22 Treble, p. 51.

23 Stedman Jones, pp. 291–3.

24 Harris, pp. 85–6.

25 Harris, p. 87.

26 J. Harris, *William Beveridge: A Biography* (Oxford, 1977), pp. 152–3.

27 Harris, *William Beveridge*, p. 285.

28 *Cd* 4499, 1909.

29 Harris, *Unemployment and Politics*, p. 346.

V Interwar Unemployment: A New Dimension

1 Sean Glynn and Alan Booth, 'Unemployment in the Interwar Period: A Case for Relearning the Lessons of the 1930s?', *Economic History Review*, 36 (1983).

2 S. Glynn and J. Oxborrow, *Interwar Britain* (1976), pp. 14–19.

3 A. Sked, *Britain's Decline: Problems and Perspectives* (Oxford, 1987).

4 N. F. R. Crafts, *British Economic Growth during the Industrial Revolution* (Oxford, 1985).

5 M. W. Kirby, *The Decline of British Economic Power Since 1870* (1981).

6 D. H. Aldcroft, *The Inter-War Economy* (1970), p. 13.

7 A. Booth and S. Glynn, 'Unemployment in the Interwar Period: A Multiple Problem', *Journal of Contemporary History*, 10 (1975), p. 621.

8 Education is examined in this series by M. Sanderson, *Education Opportunity and Social Change in England* (1988).

9 M. J. Wiener, *English Culture and the Decline of the Industrial Spirit, 1850–1980* (1985).

10 P. L. Payne, *Entrepreneurship in 19th Century Britain* (1974); D. McClosky, *Enterprise and Trade in Victorian Britain: Essays in Historical Economics* (1981).

11 M. Stewart, *Keynes and After*, 2nd edn (Harmondsworth, 1972).

12 Booth and Glynn, *Journal of Contemporary History*.

13 T. J. Hatton, 'The Outlines of a Keynesian Solution', in S. Glynn and A. E. Booth, *The Road to Full Employment* (1987).

14 D. K. Benjamin and L. A. Kochin, 'Searching for an Explanation of Unemployment in Inter-War Britain', *Journal of Political Economy*, 87 (1979).

15 F. Capie, 'Unemployment and Real Wages', in Glynn and Booth, *The Road to Full Employment*.

16 S. Broadberry, 'Unemployment in Interwar Britain: A Disequilibrium Approach', *Oxford Economic Papers*, 35 (1983).

17 Glynn and Oxborrow, pp. 157–8.

18 Glynn and Booth, *The Road to Full Employment*, p. 14.

19 C. Forster (ed.), *Australian Economic Development in the Twentieth Century* (1970).

20 D. H. Aldcroft, *The British Economy between the Wars* (Oxford, 1983).

21 N. von Tunzelmann, 'Britain 1900–45: A Survey', in R. C. Floud and D. N. McCloskey (eds.), *The Economic History of Britain since 1700*, vol. 11 (Cambridge, 1981), p. 246–8.

22 Glynn and Oxborrow, ch. 7.

23 D. H. Aldcroft, *The British Economy*: vol. 1, *The Years of Turmoil, 1920–1957* (Brighton, 1986), pp. 84–118.

24 Booth and Glynn, *Journal of Contemporary History*.

25 J. R. Shackleton, 'Economists and Unemployment', *National Westminster Bank Quarterly Review*, 2 (1982), pp. 13–29.

26 Benjamin and Kochin, *Journal of Political Economy*, 87, 1979.

27 For a fuller discussion see a companion volume in this series: A. Digby, *British Welfare Policy: Workhouse to Workfare* (1989), ch. III.

28 Quoted by J. Harris, *Unemployment and Politics* (Oxford, 1972), p. 76.

29 G. Peden, *British Economic and Social Policy: Lloyd George to Margaret Thatcher* (Oxford, 1985), pp. 36–75.

30 A. Deacon, 'Systems of Interwar Unemployment Relief', in Glynn and Booth, *The Road to Full Employment*.

31 B. B. Gilbert, *British Social Policy, 1914–1939* (1970).
32 Deacon in Glynn and Booth, *The Road to Full Employment*, p. 41.

VI Full Employment

1 A. Booth, 'The War and the White Paper', in S. Glynn and A. E. Booth, *The Road to Full Employment* (1987), p. 178.
2 R. Jones, *Wages and Employment Policy, 1936–1985* (1987), p. 19.
3 H. L. Smith (ed.), *War and Social Change: British Society in the Second World War* (Manchester, 1986), pp. x–xi.
4 J. Harris, *William Beveridge: A Biography* (Oxford, 1977).
5 I am grateful to Alan Booth for this point.
6 S. Glynn and A. E. Booth, *The Road to Full Employment* (1987), p. 188.
7 HMSO, *Employment Policy*, Cmd 6527 (1944), p. 3.
8 R. Lowe, 'Labour Policy', in Glynn and Booth, *The Road to Full Employment*.
9 Glynn and Booth, p. 189.
10 Sir Alec Cairncross, 'The Postwar Years, 1945–77', in R. C. Floud and D. N. McClosky (eds.), *Economic History of Britain since 1700* (Cambridge, 1981), vol. 2, p. 374.
11 D. N. Chester (ed.), *Lessons of the British War Economy* (1951).
12 W. H. Beveridge, *Full Employment in a Free Society* (1944).
13 J. C. R. Dow, *The Management of the British Economy, 1945–60* (Cambridge, 1964).
14 A. Maddison, *Economic Growth in the West* (1964).
15 S. Pollard, *The Wasting of the British Economy*, 2nd edn. (1982).
16 A. W. Phillips, 'The Relationship between Unemployment and the Rate of Change of Money Wages in the United Kingdom, 1861–1957', *Economica*, XXV (November 1958).
17 S. Pollard, *The Development of the British Economy*, 3rd edn. (1983), p. 263.
18 Jones, *Wages and Employment Policy*.
19 D. Maki and Z. A. Spindler, 'The Effect of Unemployment Compensation on the Rate of Unemployment in Great Britain', *Oxford Economic Papers*, 27 (1975).
20 J. J. Hughes, 'How Should We Measure Unemployment?', *British Journal of Industrial Relations*, XIII, 3 (1975).
21 Jones, p. 104.

VII Unemployment and Policy

1 S. Glynn, 'Real Policy Options', in S. Glynn and A. E. Booth, *The Road to Full Employment* (1987).

2 B. Eichengreen (ed.), *The Gold Standard in Theory and History* (1985), pp. 1–35; D. E. Moggridge, *British Monetary Policy, 1924–1931: The Norman Conquest of $4.86* (Cambridge, 1972).

3 G. Peden, *British Economic and Social Policy: Lloyd George to Margaret Thatcher* (Oxford, 1985), ch. 4.

4 M. W. Kirby, 'Industrial Policy', in Glynn and Booth.

5 A. Booth and M. Pack, *Employment, Capital and Economic Policy: Great Britain, 1918–1939* (Oxford, 1985), pp. 6–34.

6 M. Thomas, 'Rearmament and Economic Recovery in the late 1930s', *Economic History Review*, 36 (1983).

7 S. Glynn and P. G. A. Howells, 'Unemployment in the 1930s: The "Keynesian Solution" Reconsidered', *Australian Economic History Review*, 20 (1980).

8 R. Middleton, *Towards the Managed Economy: Keynes, the Treasury and the Fiscal Policy Debate of the 1930s* (1985).

9 Cmd. 3331, *Memoranda on Certain Proposals Relating to Unemployment*, BPP 1928–9, vol. XVI, pp. 873–926.

10 G. Peden, *Keynes, the Treasury and British Economic Policy* (Houndmills, 1988); R. Skidelsky, *John Maynard Keynes: Hopes Betrayed, 1883–1920* (1983); D. E. Moggridge, *Keynes* (1976).

11 For a general account of these developments see M. Bleaney, *The Rise and Fall of Keynesian Economics* (1985).

12 A. Leijonhufvud, *On Keynesian Economics and the Economics of Keynes* (Oxford, 1968); R. W. Clower, 'The Keynesian Counter-revolution: A Theoretical Reappraisal', in F. Hahn and F. Brechling (eds.), *The Theory of Interest Rates* (1965).

13 Reported in *The Times*, 29 September 1976.

14 K. Smith, *The Rise and Fall of Monetarism* (1987).

15 G. Davies, *Governments Can Affect Employment* (Employment Institute, 1985), p. 10.

16 M. Friedman, 'The Role of Monetary Policy', *American Economic Review*, LVIII (1968).

17 Davies, pp. 27–35.

18 J. J. Hughes and P. Perlman, *The Economics of Unemployment: A Comparative Analysis of Britain and the United States* (Brighton, 1984), p. 54.

19 N. Lawson, 'The British Experiment', Fifth Mais Lecture (1984).

20 S. Glynn and A. Booth, *British Unemployment in the Interwar Period: Survey and Perspective* (Canberra, 1983), pp. 24–5.

21 Peden, *British Economic and Social Policy*, pp. 85–123.

22 K. Smith, *The British Economic Crisis* (1984), pp. 113–86.

23 S. Milne, 'The Revolution of Rational Expectations', *Guardian*, 12 January 1987.
24 R. Layard, *How to Beat Unemployment* (Oxford, 1986); Davies.
25 S. Brittan, *Second Thoughts Are Full Employment Policy* (1975).
26 K. Smith, pp. 86–104.
27 W. Keegan, *Mrs Thatcher's Economic Experiment* (1984), p. 53.
28 For an interesting exception see T. Hazeldene, *Full Employment without Inflation: Manifesto for a Governed Economy* (1984).
29 G. Routh, *Unemployment: Economic Perspectives* (1986), p. 34.
30 W. Beveridge, *Full Employment in a Free Society* (1944), p. 16.

VIII Thatcher's Economic Miracle

1 House of Commons, 24 January 1978; *The Times*, 25 January 1978.
2 W. Keegan, *Mrs Thatcher's Economic Experiment* (1984).
3 In January 1958, Thorneycroft and his Treasury team resigned in protest against rising public expenditure. R. Jones, *Wages and Employment Policy 1936–1985* (1987), p. 55.
4 This speech of 4 September 1974 should be regarded as a major landmark in British economic policy. Reported in full in *The Times*, 6 September 1974.
5 OECD, *Economic Outlook* (1985).
6 G. Therborn, *Why Some Peoples Are More Unemployed than Others: The Strange Paradox of Growth and Unemployment* (1986), p. 23.
7 Therborn, p. 30.
8 W. Keegan, p. 20; see also W. Keegan, *Britain without Oil* (1985).
9 M. Crick, *Scargill and the Miners* (1985).
10 S. Glynn and S. Shaw, 'Wage Bargaining and Unemployment', *Political Quarterly*, 52 (1981).
11 G. Peden, *British Economic and Social Policy: Lloyd George to Margaret Thatcher* (Oxford, 1985), p. 92.
12 S. Glynn and J. Oxborrow, *Interwar Britain* (1976).
13 S. Glynn, 'Real Policy Options', in S. Glynn and A. E. Booth, *The Road to Full Employment* (1987).
14 S. Glynn and S. Shaw, 'Wage Bargaining and Unemployment', in B. Crick (ed.), *Unemployment* (1981).
15 A. Digby, *British Welfare Policy: Workhouse to Workfare* (1989), ch. VII.
16 Demands for workfare-type solutions continued: M. Heseltine, *Where There's a Will* (1987), p. 245.
17 Christopher Hulme, *Guardian*, 11 September 1986.
18 N. F. R. Crafts, *British Economic Growth Before and After 1979: A Review of the Evidence* (1988), table 1, p. 2.

Bibliography

Place of publication is London unless stated.

Addison, J. T. and Siebert, W. S., *The Market for Labour*, Santa Monica, 1979.

Addison, P., *The Road to 1945*, 1977.

Aldcroft, D., *Full Employment: The Elusive Goal*, Brighton, 1984.

Alison, W. P., *Observations on the Management of the Poor in Scotland*, 1840.

Arndt, H. W., *The Economic Lessons of the 1930s*, 1944.

Ashton, D. N., *Unemployment under Capitalism*, Brighton, 1986.

Astor, J. J., *et al.*, *The Third Winter of Unemployment*, 1923.

Bakke, E., *The Unemployed Man*, 1933.

Bank of England Academic Panel, 'Employment, the Real Wage and Unemployment in the UK', 24, 1984.

– 'The recovery in Britain in the 1930s', 23, 1984.

Barro, R. J., *Macroeconomics*, Chichester, 1984.

– and Grossman, H., *Money, Employment and Inflation*, Cambridge, 1976.

Bean, Charles, *et al.* (eds.), *The Rise in Unemployment*, Oxford, 1986.

Becker, G. S., *The Economics of Discrimination* 2nd edn., Chicago, 1971.

Beckerman, W. (ed.), *Wage Rigidity and Unemployment*, 1986.

Bell, D., *The Coming of Post-industrial Society*, 1974.

– and Kristol, I. (eds.), *The Crisis in Economic Theory*, New York, 1981.

Benjamin, D. K. and Kochin, L. A., 'Searching for an Explanation for Unemployment in Interwar Britain', *Journal of Political Economy*, 87, 3, 1979.

Beveridge, W. H., *A Problem of Industry*, 1909.

– *Causes and Cures of Unemployment*, 1931.

– *Social Insurance and Allied Services*, Cmd. 6404, 1942.

– *Full Employment in a Free Society*, 1944.

Bleaney, M. F., *Under Consumption Theories*, 1976.

– *The Rise and Fall of Keynesian Economics*, 1985.

Blackaby, F. (ed.), *De-Industrialisation*, 1979.

Booth, A. E. and Glynn, S., 'Unemployment in the Interwar Period: A Multiple Problem', *Journal of Contemporary History*, X, 1975.

Booth, A., 'An Administrative Experiment in Unemployment Policy in the Thirties', *Public Administration*, 56, 1978.

– 'Corporatism, Capitalism and Depression in Twentieth Century Britain', *British Journal of Sociology*, 33, 1982.

– 'The "Keynesian Revolution" in Economic Policy-Making', *Economic History Review*, 36, 1983.

– and Pack, M., *Employment, Capital and Economic Policy: Great Britain 1918–1939*, Oxford, 1985.

Box, S. and Hale, C., 'Economic Crisis and the Rising Prisoner Population in England and Wales', *Crime and Social Justice*, 17, Summer, 1982.

Branca, P. 'A New Perspective on Women's Work: A Comparative Typology', *Journal of Social History*, 9, 2, 1975.

Brierley, W., *Means Test Men*, 1935.

Brittan, S., *The Role and Limits of Government*, Houndslow, 1983.

– *Second Thoughts on Full Employment Policy*, 1975.

Broadberry, S. N., 'Unemployment in Inter-war Britain: A Disequilibrium Approach', *Oxford Economic Papers*, 35, 1983.

– 'Was the Collapse of British Industry after the World War Inevitable?', Warwick, 1988.

Brown, A. J., *World Inflation since 1950*, Cambridge, 1985.

Brown, K. D., *Labour and Unemployment, 1900–1914*, Newton Abbott, 1971.

Bruno, M. and Sachs, J., *The Economics of Worldwide Stagflation*, Oxford, 1985.

Burns, E. M., *British Unemployment Programs, 1920–35*, Washington, 1941.

Bythell, D., *The Handloom Weavers*, Cambridge, 1969.

Cain, G., 'The Challenge of Segmented Labour Market Theory to Orthodox Theory: A Survey', *Journal of Economic Literature*, 1976.

Cairncross, F. (ed.), *Changing Perceptions of Economic Policy*, 1981.

Capie, F., *Depression and Protectionism*, 1983.

Carter, A. M., *Theory of Wages and Employment*, Illinois, 1959.

Casson, M., *Youth Unemployment*, 1979.

– *The Economics of Unemployment: A Historical Perspective*, Oxford, 1983.

Chapman, S. J. and Hallsworth, H. M., *Unemployment: The Results of an Investigation Made in Lancashire and an Examination of the Poor Law Commission*, Manchester, 1909.

Clark, Colin, *National Income and Outlay*, 1937.

– *The Conditions of Economic Progress*, 1940.

– 'Do Trade Unions Raise Wages?', *Journal of Economic Affairs*, 1981.

Clarke, Roger, *Work in Crisis: The Dilemma of a Nation*, Edinburgh, 1982.

Cmnd 9474, *Employment: The Challenge to the Nation*, HMSO, 1985.

Colander, D. C., *Solutions to Unemployment*, New York, 1981.

Cole, K. *et al.*, *Why Economists Disagree*, Harlow, 1983.

Constantine, Stephen, *Unemployment in Britain between the Wars*, Harlow, 1980.

Cooper, C. M. and Clark, J. A., *Employment, Economics and Technology: The Impact of Technical Change on the Labour Market*, Brighton, 1982.

Crafts, N. F. R., *British Economic Growth Before and After 1979: A Review of the Evidence*, Centre for Economic Policy Research, 1988.

Creedy, J. (ed.), *The Economics of Unemployment in Britain*, 1981.

Crick, B., *Unemployment*, 1981.

Croucher, R., *We Refuse to Starve in Silence: A History of the NUWM, 1920–46*, London, 1987.

Davidson, R. C., *The Unemployed*, 1929.

Davies, G., *Governments Can Affect Employment*, Employment Institute, London, 1985.

Deacon, Alan, *In Search of the Scrounger*, Leeds, 1976.

Department of Employment, *Gazette* (monthly).

– *British Labour Statistics Historical Abstract, 1880–1968*, HMSO, London, 1971.

– and DHSS, *Payment of Benefits to Unemployed People*, HMSO, 1981.

Dimsdale, N. H., 'Employment and Real Wages in the Inter-war Period', *National Institute Economic Review*, 110, 1984.

Doeringer, P. and Piore, M. J., *Internal Labour Markets and Manpower Analysis*, Lexington, 1971.

– *Industrial Relations in International Perspective*, 1981.

Dornbusch, R., *Sound Currency and Full Employment*, 1985.

Dow, J. C. R., *The Management of the British Economy, 1945–60*, Cambridge, 1964.

Drage, G., *The Unemployed*, 1894.

Economist Intelligence Unit, *Coping with Unemployment*, 1982.

Edwards, R. C. *et al*, *Labour Market Segmentation*, Lexington, Mass., 1975.

Eichengreen, B., 'Juvenile Unemployment in 20th Century Britain: The Emergence of a Problem', *Social Research*, 54, 1987.

– 'Unemployment in Interwar Britain: Dole or Doledrums?', *Oxford Economic Papers*, 39, 1988.

– 'Unemployment in Interwar Britain', *Refresh*, 8, Spring, 1989.

– and Hatton, T. J. (eds.), *Interwar Unemployment in International Perspective*, The Hague, 1988.

Eisenberg, P. and Lazarsfeld, 'The Psychological Effects of Unemployment', *Psychological Bulletin*, 35, 6, June 1938.

Feiling, K., *The Life of Neville Chamberlain*, 1946.

Feinstein, C. H., *National Income Output and Expenditure in the United Kingdom, 1855–1965*, Cambridge, 1972.

– *Statistical Tables of National Income, Expenditure and Output of the United Kingdom, 1855–1965*, Cambridge, 1976.

Fineman, S., *White-Collar Unemployment: Impact and Stress*, New York, 1983.

Floud, R. and McCloskey, D. (eds.), *The Economic History of Britain since 1700*: vol. 11, *1860 to the 1970s*, Cambridge, 1981.

Francis, L. J., *Young and Unemployed*, 1984.

Friedman, M., *Essays in Positive Economics*, Chicago, 1953.

– *Studies in the Quantity Theory of Money*, Chicago, 1956.

– *The Theory of the Consumption Function*, Princeton, 1957.

– 'The Role of Monetary Policy', *American Economic Review*, 58, 1968.

– 'Unemployment versus Inflation', *IEA Occasional Papers*, 44, 1975.

– and Schwartz, A. J., *A Monetary History of the USA, 1867–1960*, Princeton, 1963.

Garraty, J. A., *Unemployment in History*, New York, 1978.

Garside, W. R., *The Measurement of Unemployment*, Oxford, 1980.

Gershuny, J. I. and Miles, I. D., *The New Service Economy: The Transformation of Employment in Industrial Societies*, 1983.

Gilbert, B. B., *The Evolution of National Insurance in Britain*, 1966.

– *British Social Policy, 1914–1939*, 1970.

Glynn, S. and Booth, A., 'Unemployment in the Interwar Period: A Multiple Problem', *Journal of Contemporary History*, 10, 4, 1975.

– 'Interwar Unemployment: Restatement and Comments', *Journal of Contemporary History*, 15, 4, 1980.

– 'Interwar Unemployment: Two Views', *Journal of Contemporary History*, 17, 3, 1982.

– 'Unemployment in the Interwar Period: A Case for Relearning the Lessons of the 1930s?', *Economic History Review*, 36, 1983.

– 'British Unemployment in the Interwar Period: Survey and Perspective', *Working Papers in Economic History*, No. 16, Australian National University, August 1983.

– 'Building Counterfactual Pyramids', *Economic History Review*, XXXVIII, 1, 1985.

– (eds.), *The Road to Full Employment* (1986).

Glynn, S. and Howells, P. G. A., 'Unemployment in the 1930s: The

"Keynesian Solution" Reconsidered', *Australian Economic History Review*, 20, 1980.

Glynn, S. and Oxborrow, J., *Interwar Britain: A Social and Economic History*, 1976.

Glynn, S. and Shaw, S., 'Wage Bargaining and Unemployment', *Political Quarterly*, 52, 1981.

Godfrey, M., *Global Unemployment: The New Challenge to Economic Theory*, Brighton, 1986.

Gordon, A., *Redundancy in the 1980s: The Take-up of the Voluntary Schemes*, IMS, 1984.

Gowland, D., *Inflation and Unemployment*, Brighton, 1985.

Greenhalgh, C. A. *et al.* (ed.), *The Causes of Unemployment*, Oxford, 1983.

Greenwood, W., *Love on the Dole*, 1933.

Gunderson, Morley, *et al.* (eds.), *Unemployment: International Perspectives*, Toronto, 1987.

Hahn, F. H. and Brechling, F. P. R., *The Theory of Interest Rates*, 1965.

Handy, C., *The Future of Work: A Guide to a Changing Society*, Oxford, 1984.

Hannington, W., *Unemployed Struggles, 1919–1936*, 1936.

– *The Problems of the Distressed Areas*, 1937.

Harris, J., *Unemployment and Politics*, Oxford, 1972.

– *William Beveridge*, Oxford, 1977.

Harrod, R., *The Life of John Maynard Keynes*, 1952.

Hatton, T. J., 'Unemployment Benefits and the Macro-Economics of the Interwar Labour Market: A Further Analysis', *Oxford Economic Papers*, 35, 182, 1983.

– 'Unemployment in the 1930s and the "Keynesian Solution": Some Notes of Dissent', *Australian Economic History Review*, 25, 1985.

Hawkins, K., *Unemployment*, 1979.

Hayek, F. A., *Prices and Production*, 1935.

– *1980s Unemployment and the Unions*, IEA, 1980.

Hayes, J. and Nutman, P., *Understanding the Unemployed: The Psychological Effects of Unemployment*, 1981.

Hazeldene, Tim, *Full Employment without Inflation: Manifesto for a Governed Economy*, 1984.

Heseltine, M., *Where There's a Will*, 1987.

Hicks, J. *The Crisis in Keynesian Economics*, Oxford, 1972.

HM Treasury, *The Relationship between Employment and Wages*, 1985.

HMSO, *Memorandum on Certain Proposals Relating to Unemployment*, Cmd. 3331, 1929.

– *Employment Policy*, Cmd. 6527, 1944.

Hobson, J. A., *The Problem of the Unemployed*, 1896.
- *The Economics of Unemployment*, 1922.
Howson, S., *Domestic Monetary Management in Britain, 1919–38*, Cambridge, 1975.
- and Winch, D., *The Economic Advisory Council, 1930–9*, Cambridge, 1977.
Hughes, J. J., 'How Should We Measure Unemployment?', *British Journal of Industrial Relations*, XII, 3, 1975.
- and Perlman, R., *The Economics of Unemployment*, Brighton, 1984.
Hunter, L. C. and Mulney, C., *Economics of Wages and Labour*, 1981.
Hutchison, T. W., *A Review of Economic Doctrines, 1870–1929*, 1953.
- *Keynes versus the 'Keynesians'?*, IEA, 1977.
- *On Revolution and Progress in Economic Knowledge*, Cambridge, 1978.
- *The Politics and Philosophy of Economics*, Oxford, 1981.
Hutton, Will, *The Revolution that Never Was: An Assessment of Keynesian Economics*, 1986.
Illich, I., *The Right to Useful Employment and Its Enemies*, 1978.
Jahoda, M., *Employment and Unemployment: A Social Psychological Analysis*, Cambridge, 1982.
- et al., *Marienthal: The Geography of an Unemployed Community*, 1972.
Jenkins, C. and Sherman, B., *The Collapse of Work*, 1979.
Jennings, H., *Brynmawr: A Study of a Depressed Area*, 1934.
Jewkes, J. and Winterbottom, A., *Juvenile Unemployment*, 1933.
Johnson, C., *Measuring the Economy*, 1988.
Joll, C. (ed.), *Developments in Labour Market Analysis*, 1983.
Jones, B., *Sleepers, Wake! Technology and the Future of Work*, Brighton, 1982.
Jones, R. *Wages and Employment Policy*, 1987.
Jordon, Bill, *Mass Unemployment and the Future of Britain*, Oxford, 1982.
Kaldor, N., *The Scourge of Monetarism*, Oxford, 1982.
Katouzian, H., *Ideology and Method in Economics*, 1980.
Keane, J. and Owens, J., *After Full Employment*, 1986.
Keegan, W., *Mrs Thatcher's Economic Experiment*, 1984.
Kelvin, P. and Jarrett, J. E., *Unemployment: Its Social-Psychological Effects*, Cambridge, 1985.
Kelvin, P., 'Work as a Source of Identity: The Implications of Unemployment', *British Journal of Guidance and Counselling*, 9, 1, January 1987.
Keynes, J. M., *The Collected Writings of John Maynard Keynes*, vols. I–XXVII, 1971–80.
- *The General Theory of Employment, Interest and Money*, 1936.
- and Henderson, H., *Can Lloyd George Do It?*, 1929.
Kingsford, Peter, *The Hunger Marchers in Britain, 1920–1939*, 1982.

Bibliography

Kinnock, N., *Making Our Way*, 1986.

Knight, K. G., *Unemployment: An Economic Analysis*, Brighton, 1987.

Kumar, K., *Prophecy and Progress*, 1978.

Lawson, N., 'The British Experiment', Fifth Mais Lecture, London, 1984.

Layard, Richard, *The Causes of British Unemployment*, 1985.

– *An Incomes Policy to Help the Unemployed*, Employment Institute, 1986.

– *How to Beat Unemployment*, Oxford, 1986.

– and Nickell, S., 'The Causes of British Unemployment', National Institute Economic Review, February 1985.

Leadbeater, C. and Lloyd, J., *In Search of Work*, 1987.

Lee, C. H., *British Regional Employment Statistics, 1841–1971*, Cambridge, 1979.

Leijonhufvud, A., *On Keynesian Economics and the Economics of Keynes*, Oxford, 1968.

– *Information and Co-ordination: Essays in Macroeconomic Theory*, Oxford, 1981.

Lekachman, R., *The Age of Keynes*, Harmondsworth, 1967.

Lewis, W. A., *Economic Survey, 1919–1939*, 1949.

Liberal Party, *We Can Conquer Unemployment*, 1929.

London and Cambridge Economic Service, *The British Economy: Key Statistics, 1900–1966*, 1968.

Lowe, R., *Adjusting to Democracy: The Role of the Ministry of Labour in British Politics, 1916–39*, Oxford, 1986.

Lucas, R. E., *Studies in Business-Cycle Theory*, Oxford, 1981.

– and Rapping, L. A., 'Real Wages, Employment and the Price Level', *Journal of Political Economy*, LXXVII, 1969.

Macmillan, Harold, *The Middle Way*, 1938.

Macmillan Committee, *Report of the Committee on Finance and Industry*, Cmd. 3897, 1931.

Maddison, A., *Economic Growth in the West*, 1964.

– and Wilpstra, B. S. (eds.), *Unemployment – the European Perspective*, 1982.

Maki, D. and Spindler, Z. A., 'The Effect of Unemployment Compensation on the Rate of Unemployment in Great Britain', *Oxford Economic Papers*, 27, 1975.

Malinvaud, E., *The Theory of Unemployment Reconsidered*, Oxford, 1977.

– *Mass Unemployment*, Oxford, 1984.

– and Fitoussi, J. P., *Unemployment in Western Countries*, 1980.

Manning, N. (ed.), *Social Problems and Welfare Ideology*, 1985.

Marsden, David, *Workless: An Exploration of the Social Contract between Society and the Worker*, 1982.

– *The End of Economic Man?*, Brighton, 1986.

Marshall, A., *Principles of Economics*, 9th edn., 1961.

Matthews, R. C. O., 'Why Has Britain Had Full Employment since the War', in Feinstein, C. H. (ed.), *The Managed Economy: Essays in British Economic Policy and Performance Since 1929*, Oxford, 1983.

– Feinstein, C. H. and Odling-Smee, J. C., *British Economic Growth, 1856–1973*, Oxford, 1983.

Malthus, T. R., *Principles of Political Economy*, 1820.

– *An Essay on the Principle of Population as it Affects the Future Improvement of Society*, 1826, 1966 edn.

Marx, K., *Capital*, Moscow, 1961.

Metcalf, David, *Alternatives to Unemployment: Special Employment Measures in Britain*, PSI, 1982.

– *et al.*, 'Still Searching for an Explanation of Unemployment in Inter-war Britain', *Journal of Political Economy*, 90, 1982.

Middleton, R., *Towards the Managed Economy: Keynes, the Treasury and the Fiscal Policy Debate of the 1930s*, 1985.

Miller, F., 'The Unemployment Policy of the National Government, 1931–36', *Historical Journal*, 19, 1976.

Miller, R. and Wood, J. B., *What Price Unemployment? An Alternative Approach*, Hobart Paper 92, 1982.

Minford, P., *Unemployment: Cause and Cure*, Oxford, 1985.

Mitchell, M., 'The Effects of Unemployment on the Social Conditions of Women and Children', *History Workshop Journal*, 19, 1985.

Moggeridge, D. E., *British Monetary Policy, 1924–1931*, Cambridge, 1972.

Morgan, K. O., *Labour in Power, 1945–1951*, Oxford, 1984.

Mosley, P., *The Making of Economic Policy*, Brighton, 1984.

(National Insurance) *Final Report of the Royal Commission on National Insurance*, Cmd. 4185, 1932.

Nevin, E., 'The Origins of Cheap Money, 1931–32', *Economica*, n.s. XX, 1953.

Northcote, J. and Rogers, P., *Microelectronics in Industry: What's Happening in Britain*, PSI, 1982.

OECD, *Measuring Employment and Unemployment*, Paris, 1979.

– *Unemployment Compensation and Related Policy Measures*, Paris, 1979.

– *Microelectronics, Productivity and Employment*, Paris, 1981.

– *The Challenge of Unemployment*, Paris, 1982.

– *High Unemployment: A Challenge for Income Support Policies*, Paris, 1984.

Offe, C., *Disorganised Capitalism: Contemporary Transformation of Work and Politics*, Cambridge, 1985.

Office of Population, Census and Surveys, *General Household Survey*, annual.

– *Labour Force Survey*, annual.

Orwell, G., *The Road to Wigan Pier*, 1937, 1975 edn.

Pahl, R., *Divisions of Labour*, Oxford, 1984.

Patinkin, D., *Keynes's Monetary Thought: A Study in Its Development*, Durham, NC, 1976.

Peden, G. C., 'Keynes, the Treasury and Unemployment in the Later Nineteen Thirties', *Oxford Economic Papers*, 32, 1980.

– *British Economic and Social Policy: Lloyd George to Margaret Thatcher*, Deddington, 1985.

Phillips, A. W., 'The Relationship between Unemployment and the Rate of Change of Money Wage Rates in the United Kingdom', *Economica*, 25, 1958.

Pickard, T., *Jarrow March*, 1982.

Pigou, A. C., *The Theory of Unemployment*, 1933.

– *Lapses from Full Employment*, 1944.

Pilgrim Trust, *Men without Work*, Cambridge, 1938.

Piore, M. J., *Unemployment and Inflation: Institutionalist and Structuralist Views*, New York, 1979.

Pollard, S. (ed.), *The Gold Standard and Employment Policies between the Wars*, 1970.

Reid, D. A., 'The Decline of Saint Monday', *Past and Present*, 71, 1976.

Rentoul, J., *The Rich Get Richer*, 1987.

Richardson, J. and Henning, R., *Unemployment Policy Responses of Western Democracies*, 1984.

Roberts, B. *et al.* (eds.), *New Approaches to Economic Life: Economic Restructuring, Unemployment and the Social Division of Labour*, Manchester, 1985.

Robertson, J., *Futurework*, Aldershot, 1985.

Rogers, J. E. T., *Six Centuries of Work and Wages*, 1909.

Routh, G., *Unemployment: Economic Perspectives*, 1986.

Rowntree, B. S. and Lasker, B., *Unemployment: A Social Study*, 1911.

Royal Institute of International Affairs, *Unemployment: An International Problem*, 1935.

Sabel, C. F., *Work and Politics: The Division of Labour in Industry*, New York, 1982.

Samuelson, P. A., *Economics, an Introductory Analysis*, New York, 1964.

Sargent, T. J. and Wallace, N., '"Rational" Expectations, the Optional Monetary Instrument and the Optimal Money Supply Rule', *Journal of Political Economy*, LXXXIII, 1975.

Schumacher, E. F., *Good Work*, 1979.

Scott, M. and Laslett, R. A., *Can We Get Back to Full Employment*, 1978.

Seabrook, J., 'Unemployment Now and in the 1930s', *Political Quarterly*, 52, 1, Jan.–March 1981.

– *Unemployment*, 1983.

Shephard, P. M. and Barraclough, B. M., 'Work and Suicide: An Empirical Investigation', *British Journal of Psychiatry*, 136, May 1980.

Sherman, B., *Working at Leisure*, 1986.

Showler, B., 'Racial Minority Group Unemployment: Trends and Characteristics', *International Journal of Social Economics*, 7, 4, 1980.

– and Sinfield, A., *The Workless State*, Oxford, 1981.

Sinclair, P. J., *Unemployment: Economic Theory and Evidence*, Oxon, 1987.

Sinfield, A., *What Unemployment Means*, Oxford, 1981.

Sked, A., *Britain's Decline*, Oxford, 1987.

Skidelsky, R., *Politicians and the Slump: The Labour Government, 1929–31*, Harmondsworth, 1970.

– *John Maynard Keynes: Hopes Betrayed, 1883–1920*, 1983.

Smith, A., *The Wealth of Nations*, 1776, Oxford, 1976.

Smith, David, *The Rise and Fall of Monetarism*, 1987.

Smith, D. J., *Unemployment and Racial Minorities*, PSI, 1981.

Smith, K., *The British Economic Crisis*, 1984.

Smith, R., *Unemployment and Health*, Oxon, 1987.

Solow, R. M., 'On Theories of Unemployment', Presidential Address to 92nd Meeting of American Economic Association, Atlanta, 1979.

Southgate, P., 'Disturbances of July 1981 in Handsworth, Birmingham: A Survey of the Views and Experiences of Male Residents, *Public Disorder*, Home Office Research Study No. 72, HMSO, 1982.

Stedman Jones, G., *Outcast London*, Oxford, 1971.

Stevenson, J., *British Society, 1914–1945*, Harmondsworth, 1984.

– and Cook, C., *The Slump: Society and Politics during the Depression*, 1977.

Stewart, M., *Keynes and After*, 1967.

Tawney, R. H. S., *Equality*, 1964 edn.

Temin, P., *Did Monetary Forces Cause the Great Depression?*, New York, 1976.

Therborn, G., *Why Some Peoples Are More Unemployed than Others*, 1986.

Thirlwall, A. P., 'Keynesian Employment Theory Is Not Defunct', *Three Banks Review*, 131, 1981.

Thompson, E. P., 'Time, Work-Discipline and Industrial Capitalism', in Flinn, M. W. and Smout, T. C., *Essays in Social History*, Oxford, 1974.

Tomlinson, J., *Problems of British Economic Policy, 1870–1945*, 1981.

Treble, J. H., *Urban Poverty in Britain*, 1979.

Turnbull, M., 'Attitude of Government and Administration towards the Hunger Marches of the 1920s and 1930s', *Journal of Social Policy*, II, 1973.

Unemployment Unit, *Bulletin*.

Walker, S. and Barton, L., *Youth Unemployment and Schooling*, Milton Keynes, 1986.

Wallace, Claire, *For Richer for Poorer: Growing up in and out of Work*, 1987.

Waller, P. J. (ed.), *Politics and Social Change in Modern Britain*, 1987.

Walras, L., *Elements d'économie politique pure*, 1874.

Walsh, K., *Long-term Unemployment: An International Perspective*, 1987.

Walters, A., *Britain's Economic Renaissance: Margaret Thatcher's Reforms, 1979–1984*, Oxford, 1986.

Watts, A. G., *Education, Unemployment and the Future of Work*, Milton Keynes, 1983.

White, Michael (ed.), *The Social World of the Young Unemployed*, PSI, 1987.

Wiener, M. J., *English Culture and the Decline of the Industrial Spirit, 1850–1980*, Cambridge, 1981.

Wiles, P. and Routh, G., *Economics in Disarray*, Oxford, 1984.

Wilkinson, E., *The Town that Was Murdered*, 1939.

Williams, Stanley, *A Job to Live*, 1983.

Winch, D., *Economics and Policy*, 1969.

Wootton, B., *The Social Foundation of Wage Policy*, 1955.

Worswick, E. D. N. (ed.), *The Concept and Measurement of Involuntary Unemployment*, 1976.

Yuill, K. A. and Hull, C. (eds.), *Regional Policy in the European Community*, 1980.

Index